JOHN DONNE

Poetry & Prose

AMS PRESS

NEW YORK

ANNO DNI. 1591.

ÆTATIS SVÆ 18.

This was for youth, Strength, Mirth, and wit that Time
Most count their golden Age; but t'was not thine.
Thine was thy later yeares, so much refind
From youths Drosse, Mirth, & wit; as thy pure mind
Thought (like the Angels) nothing but the Praise
Of thy Creator, in those last, best Dayes.
    Witnes this Booke, (thy Emblemie) which begins
    With Love; but endes, with Sighes, & Teares for sins.

Will: Marshall sculpsit.   IZ: WA:

JOHN DONNE

Poetry & Prose

with

IZAAC WALTON'S LIFE

Appreciations by
BEN JONSON, DRYDEN, COLERIDGE
and others

With an Introduction and Notes by
H. W. GARROD

OXFORD
AT THE CLARENDON PRESS

Library of Congress Cataloging in Publication Data

Donne, John, 1572-1631.
   Poetry & prose.

   Reprint of the 1960 ed., published by the Clarendon
Press, Oxford.
   I. Walton, Izaak, 1593-1683. II. Garrod, Heathcote
William, 1878-1960. III. Donne, John, 1572-1631.
Selected works. 1976.
PR2246.G3 1976   821'.3   75-41077
ISBN 0-404-14769-0

Reprinted from an original in the collections of the
University of Chicago Library
From the edition of 1960, Oxford
First AMS edition published in 1976

Manufactured in the United States of America

AMS PRESS INC.
NEW YORK, N.Y.

CONTENTS

CONTENTS

INTRODUCTION

DONNE's reputation, like everything else about him, exhibits paradox and vicissitude. The first edition of his *Poems* appeared in 1633: in the year preceding, Shakespeare had achieved his second folio edition. If in 1633 a vote had been taken to determine who was the greatest figure in English literature, it is likely that Donne would have got more votes than Shakespeare. I am not sure that he would not have had the votes of everybody except Ben Jonson and Milton. Donne had died two years previously; and the event had not wanted the meed of melodious tears. Almost everyone brought his tribute of verse. The Muses who with words lucky and unlucky favoured the urn of Prince Henry, or, at a later date, that of Lycidas, were hardly more numerous. Among the elegists whose poems adorn the first edition of Donne's are poets as good as King and Carew, as indifferent as Corbet or Godolphin. Clarendon, more famous in prose, contributes an epitaph of which some of the phrases recall, or are recalled by, Milton's lines on Shakespeare. Dr. Busby plucks the laurel 'with forced fingers rude', praising Donne as 'the Prince of Wit' and as a preacher in whose eloquence Chrysostom lives again. Falkland, a gentler soul, pleads that only Jonson shall write Donne's epitaph, only Laud preach his funeral sermon. An elegy by Izaak Walton praises 'miraculous Donne'; first for the miracle of a love-poetry wherein 'was all Philosophie', and then for the miracle of the poet's repentance, leading to repentance others—among them his 'convert' Walton. The poem deserves the place it has in some editions of Walton's *Life* of Donne (though I cannot find it, where Grierson finds it, in the edition of 1658). Not the poem, however, but the *Life* is Walton's 'best piece of poetry'. Of Donne's last years it is, as Grierson calls it, 'the adequate and perfect record'. For the earlier years it is defective in information, in accuracy and, it may be, in candour. Yet the whole fulfils the end of biography, as Walton understood it—that the writer's *love* should 'follow his friend's fame beyond death and the forgetful grave'.

Ben Jonson wished to hang Donne for the blasphemy of 'not keeping the accent', and for the lesser blasphemy of writing about Elizabeth Drury as though she were the Virgin Mary. It is likely that Milton thought little of Donne. Even so, there are early poems of Milton where you may catch him out being 'metaphysical'. We know, moreover, that he thought Cowley, after Shakespeare and Spenser, the greatest of our poets; and the fame of Cowley, over several generations, bore up that of Donne. Cowley, like Donne, tended to blaspheme the accent; and like Donne (and Ben Jonson too), he preferred 'plain English' to poetic diction. But when Waller and Denham had refined our numbers, and when 'poetic diction' came with Dryden—'there was before Dryden no poetical diction', Dr. Johnson says, plumply— the fame of Donne's poetry suffered decline. Dryden speaks of him as 'the greatest wit, though not the greatest poet of our nation'. Dr. Johnson, in his *Dictionary*, shows a rather notable fondness for him; but in his *Life* of Cowley, while allowing him the merit of 'a man of very extensive and varied learning', he, in effect, denies to him both wit and poetry. Hazlitt, lecturing on the English Poets early in 1818, is content to 'know nothing' of Donne except, apparently, the scraps quoted by Dr. Johnson. Later, he got to know him better; but never to the point of sympathy or understanding. Some of Hazlitt's friends were better informed and more discerning. Lamb praised both Donne and Cowley for a 'warmth of soul and generous feeling' which 'forty thousand natural poets' could not equal.

Coleridge praised them for what is still one of their first merits, their good and pure English; and he speaks finely of Donne's 'wonder-exciting vigour, intenseness, and peculiarity'. He extols *The Extasie* in terms sufficiently ecstatic to create the suspicion that he gave to the poem an interpretation more spiritual than it can well bear. To De Quincey, again, Donne appeared 'one of the subtlest intellects that England has produced'. But these men are virtuosos, hunting the rare and neglected; and it was not until near the beginning of the present century that Donne began to recover that fullness of poetical repute which he had enjoyed before the Restoration.

If I were asked why to-day so many persons who do not know good from bad read so good a poet as Donne—and the more easily where he is most difficult—I should be inclined to assign as one reason for it our New Psychology. While we are still waiting for a good *Life* of Donne, the *Songs and Sonets*, the Elegies, and Donne's early poems generally, have yielded to psychological investigation a wealth of biographical material which more than compensates the reticence of Walton—indeed, if Walton had not been reticent at all, he could hardly have told us as much about Donne as we have been able to discover without him.

The New Psychology has helped Donne. He has been assisted also, I fancy, by some recent tendencies in religious thought. His *Divine Poems*, which, to myself at least, seem far less divine than the secular ones, and which a considered criticism might reasonably rank below the best of Crashaw, make a rather special appeal to Anglo-Catholic thought and feeling. Those poems, moreover—and Donne's poems generally—are now widely read (as is proper) in connexion with Donne's Sermons. The Sermons elevate Donne, in the opinion of some good critics, to a place among the great orators. If it is not in flesh and blood to wish the Eighty

Sermons to be ninety, nor the Fifty fifty-five, at least they can no longer be neglected.

Grierson, to whom our study of Donne owes so much, warned us, long ago, against 'cutting Donne's life across'; against separating too sharply the early Donne from the Donne of the *Divine Poems*. Mr. T. S. Eliot goes even a little farther. 'Nobody now, I suppose,' he writes, 'divides Donne's life into two periods, one dissolute and irreligious, the other a revulsion to intense and austere piety.' It is only poor Donne himself who does that. He alone knows of two Donnes. *We*, Mr. Eliot says, 'agree that it is one and the same man in both early and later life'. 'Nor can I take very seriously', he adds, 'Donne's later remorse or repentance.' Perhaps, in any case, the real problem is, not that of two Donnes, but of a number almost infinite. 'Miraculous Donne', as Walton calls him, may be thought chiefly miraculous in that order of miracle which he was never tired of praising—variety:

> Change is the nursery
> Of musicke, joy, life, and eternity

He is most himself when he is never the same for two minutes together. That, perhaps, is why his best miracle must ever be the *Songs and Sonets*. Others of his poems men will not willingly let die. From *Divine Poems* they will save 'Death, be not proud . . .' and 'Wilt thou forgive that sinne . . .?'. From the twelfth Elegy they will keep these lines:

> I will not look upon the quickening Sun,
> But straight her beauty to my sense shall run;
> The ayre shall note her soft, the fire most pure;
> Water suggest her clear, and the earth sure.
> Time shall not lose her passages; the Spring
> How fresh our love was in the beginning;
> The Summer how it ripened in the eare;
> And Autumn what our golden harvests were.

'Time shall not lose *these* passages'—and others. But it will
be by *Songs and Sonets* that Donne will be ultimately
approved:

> By these hymnes men shall approve
> Us *Canoniz'd* for Love.

These 'hymnes' will find an approval a good deal different,
perhaps, from that which salutes them to-day; they will be
read in a more disinterested fashion.

To a more disinterested study of them an invitation is
furnished by an essay of M. Pierre Legouis. M. Legouis in-
vites us to study *Songs and Sonets*, not as a record of Donne's
love-affairs, 'except in the most general terms', and not
as 'fragments of a metaphysical creed or system', but as
examples of art, of an art characterized by a singular boldness and originality. While he does not go so far as to say
that the *Songs and Sonets* are just 'dramatic lyrics', M.
Legouis reminds us that at least one of them is spoken in
the person of a woman; and in general, 'what earnestness
there is', he says, in these poems, 'often belongs, not to the
poet himself, but to the character he presents, and to the
situation in which he places this character'. The poems are
only so far autobiographic as every poet necessarily talks
about himself, and out of himself. You will as easily write
the *Life* of Donne from *Songs and Sonets* as you will write
the *Life* of Elizabeth Drury out of *The Anatomie of the World*.
In the wealth of scholastic divinity, again, with which Donne
adorns his eroticism, M. Legouis does not find that pure
enthusiasm for theoretical truth which some critics have
fancied themselves to discern. In the mere externals of art,
Donne's variety and boldness are strikingly brought home
to us by the observation that in *Songs and Sonets* he employs
no less than forty-six different stanza-forms, of which forty-
two seem to be his own invention. That in the development
of feeling he is sometimes hampered by the intricacy of his

own metrical forms is perhaps true. But few persons will agree with M. Legouis when he contends that most of the *Songs and Sonets* begin in feeling and degenerate into mere triviality of dialectic—that, as they grow, they lose poetry. So far is this not true that, in fact, almost none of Donne's greatest, and most feeling, lines belong to his initial stanzas. It is, however, true that one or two of his finest successes are written in familiar metres:

> As 'twixt two equal Armies, Fate
>   Suspends uncertaine victorie,
> Our soules, (which to advance their state,
>   Were gone out,) hung 'twixt her, and mee,
>
> And whil'st our soules negotiate there,
>   Wee like sepulchrall statues lay;
> All day, the same our postures were,
>   And we said nothing, all the day.

That is from *The Extasie*—that crowning glory of *Songs and Sonets*. Or take this, from *A Feaver*:

> Oh do not die, for I shall hate
>   All women so, when thou art gone,
> That thee I shall not celebrate,
>   When I remember, thou wast one.

These simpler measures Donne uses, in his own manner, supremely. But not by preference, nor often; and to ask why is to stumble upon that character of his art which marks him off from all other poets. He felt these simpler measures to contain a real peril for him. Using them, he was in too much danger of happening upon the purely beautiful; and for the purely beautiful he has, whether as a lover or as an artist, something like a positive distaste. Just as his philosophy of love is summed in the doctrine that the lover has nothing to do with beauty or virtue—

> if we
> Make love to woman, virtue is not shee,
> As beauty's not . . .

—so his philosophy of poetry rests in the faith that the conventional elements of the beautiful—symmetry, proportion, colour of words, and the effects of melody—are a barrier between the poet and reality. 'Love built on beauty, soone as beauty dies'; and the same is true of poetry. For the chivalric Petrarchian conception of both—'the fantastic strain of new-touch'd youth'—Donne substitutes a theory and practice rough and sceptical; as though the pure satisfactions of love and poetry were to be sought only in some positive uncomeliness. If he indulges here and there a gentler manner, it is with a self-ashamed impatience. 'For God's sake hold your tongue . . .', 'Love, any devil else but you . . .', 'Busy old foole . . .'—these, and not gentler phrases, are his characteristic preludes.

In *Songs and Sonets* Donne addressed himself very deliberately to a miracle never before essayed—to create a love-poetry which should respect almost nothing that poetry had respected hitherto: neither beauty, nor tenderness, nor words, nor melody. That he should respect respectability was not asked of him. Donne, the young Donne, had a solid respect for nothing else in the world except pure passion. To the justification of passion he fetches from the remote corners of the imagination every extravagance of analogue, all the ingenuity of his preposterous dialectic. He ends by creating a poetry in which the distinction between poetry and prose is only half-preserved; yet a poetry which is its own miracle; for whatever the source of its effects, it succeeds in making all other poetry appear less deadly earnest.

DONNE'S LIFE

1571. Born in London (?Aug. 16).

1575. John Donne, the poet's father, dies, Jan. 16.

1584. Matriculated at Oxford, from Hart Hall, Oct. 23.

1584–7. At Oxford.

1587–90. At Cambridge.

1591. Student at Thavies Inn.

1592. Entered at Lincoln's Inn, May 6.

1592–Nov. 1594. At Lincoln's Inn.

1593. Henry Donne, the poet's brother, arrested in May for harbouring a seminary priest, dies shortly afterwards in Newgate.

      23 June, Donne admitted to his share in his father's estate.

1594. April, Donne admitted to his share of Henry Donne's estate.

1595–6. Travelling in Italy and Spain.

1596. Takes part in Essex's expedition against Cadiz.

1597. Takes part in the Islands expedition.

1598–1602. Secretary to Sir Thomas Egerton.

1601. Marries Ann More (December). Dismissed by Sir Thomas Egerton.

1602. Imprisoned in the Fleet (February).

1602–4. Living with his wife at Pyrford, as the guest of Sir Francis Wooley.

1606–7. Living at Mitcham (with lodgings in the Strand, London); working for Thomas Morton.

1607. Morton appointed Dean of Gloucester (June 22); urges Donne to take orders, offering to provide him with a benefice.

      Donne contributes prefatory verses to Jonson's *Volpone*.

1608. Engaged on the composition of the *Biathanatos*.

1610. *Pseudo-Martyr* published. Donne receives Hon. M.A. from the University of Oxford.

1611. Published *Ignatius his Conclave*: and *The Anatomie of the World*.

1611 (Nov.)–1612 (Sept.). With Sir Robert Drury in France and the Low Countries.

1615. Takes Holy Orders (Jan. 23).

      Receives, by request of the King, Hon. D.D. from the University of Cambridge (April).

      Preaches before the Queen at Greenwich, April 30.

      Becomes vicar of Keyston and Sevenoaks.

1616. Appointed Reader in Divinity to Lincoln's Inn (October).

1617. Death of his wife, Ann.

1619 (May)–1620. Attached to Viscount Doncaster's mission to Germany.

1621. Appointed Dean of St. Paul's (Nov. 19).

1624. Appointed vicar of St. Dunstan's; published *Devotions upon Emergent Occasions*.

1631. Preaches before the King the Sermon known as *Death's Duell* (Feb. 12). Dies in London, March 31.

IZAAC WALTON

The Life and Death of Dr *Donne,*
late Deane of St Pauls London.

IF that great Master of Language and Art, Sir *Henry Woot-
ton*, Provost of Eaton Colledge, (lately deceased) had lived
to see the publication of these Sermons, he had presented the
world with the Authors life exactly written. It was a Work
worthy his undertaking, and he fit to undertake it; betwixt whom and our Author, there was such a friendship
contracted in their youths, that nothing but death could
force the separation. And though their bodies were divided,
that learned Knights love followed his friends fame beyond
the forgetfull grave, which he testified by intreating me 10
(whom he acquainted with his designe) to inquire of certaine
particulars that concerned it: Not doubting but my knowledge of the Author, and love to his memory, would make
my diligence usefull. I did prepare them in a readiness to
be augmented, and rectified by his powerfull pen, but then
death prevented his intentions.

When I heard that sad newes, and likewise that these
Sermons were to be publisht without the Authors life,
(which I thought was rare) indignation or griefe (I know
not whether) transported me so far, that I re-viewed my 20
forsaken Collections, and resolved the world should see the
best picture of the Author that my artlesse Pensil (guided by
the hand of Truth) could present to it.

If I be demanded, as once *Pompeys* poore Bondman was,[1]
(whilest he was alone on the Sea shore gathering the pieces
of an old Boat to burne the body of his dead Master) What

[1] *Plutarch.*

art thou that preparest the funeralls of *Pompey* the great?
Who I am that so officiously set the Authors memorie on
fire? I hope the question hath in it more of wonder then
disdaine.

Wonder indeed the Reader may, that I (who professe my
selfe artlesse) should presume with my faint light to shew
forth his life, whose very name makes it illustrious; but be
this to the disadvantage of the person represented, certaine
I am, it is much to the advantage of the beholder; who shall
10 see the Authors picture in a naturall dresse, which ought to
beget faith in what is spoken, for he that wants skill to
deceive, may safely be trusted.

And though it may be my fortune to fall under some
censures for this undertaking, yet I am pleased in a beliefe
I have, that if the Authors glorious spirit (which is now in
heaven) can have the leasure to look downe, and see his
meanest friend in the midst of his officious duty, he will not
disdaine my well meaning sacrifice to his memory. For
whilst his conversation made me (and many others) happy
20 below, I know his humility and gentleness was eminent:
And I have heard Divines say, those vertues that are but
sparks on earth, become great and glorious flames in heaven.

He was borne in LONDON, of good and vertuous Parents;
And though his own learning and other multiplied merits,
may justly seeme sufficient to dignifie both himselfe and
posteritie; yet Reader be pleased to know, that his Father
was masculinely and lineally descended from a very ancient
Family in Wales, where many of his name now live, that have
and deserve great reputation in that Countrey.

30 By his Mother he was descended from the Family of the
famous Sir *Thomas More*, sometimes Lord Chancellor of
England; and also from that worthy and laborious Judge
Rastall, who left behind him the vast Statutes of the Lawes
of this Kingdome, most exactly abridged.

He had his first breeding in his Fathers house, where a private Tutor had the care of him, till he was nine yeares of age; he was then sent to the Universitie of Oxford, having at that time a command of the French and Latine Tongues, when others can scarce speak their owne.

There he remained in Hart Hall, (having for the advancement of his studies, Tutors in severall Sciences to instruct him) till time made him capable, and his learning exprest in many publique Exercises, declared him fit to receive his first Degree in the Schooles, which he forbore by advise from his 10 friends, who being of the Romish perswasion, were conscionably averse to some parts of the Oath, alwayes tendred and taken at those times.

About the fourteenth yeare of his age, he was transplanted from Oxford to Cambridge, where (that he might receive nourishment from both soiles) he staid till his seventeenth yeare. All which time he was a most laborious Student, often changing his studies, but endeavouring to take no Degree for the reasons formerly mentioned.

About his seventeenth yeare he was removed to London, 20 and entred into Lincolnes Inne, with an intent to study the Law, where he gave great testimonies of wit, learning, and improvement in that profession, which never served him for any use, but onely for ornament.

His Father died before his admission into that Society, and (being a Merchant) left him his Portion in money (which was 3000. li.) His Mother, and those to whose care he was committed, were watchful to improve his knowledge, and to that end appointed him there also Tutors in severall Sciences, as the Mathematicks and others, to attend and 30 instruct him. But with these Arts they were advised to instill certaine particular principles of the Romish Church, of which those Tutors (though secretly) profest themselves to be members.

They had almost obliged him to their faith, having for their advantage, besides their opportunity, the example of his most deare and pious Parents, which was a powerfull perswasion, and did work upon him, as he professeth in his PREFACE to his *Pseudo-Martyr*.

He was now entred into the nineteenth yeare of his age, and being unresolved in his Religion, (though his youth and strength promised him a long life) yet he thought it necessary to rectifie all scruples which concerned that: And therefore
10 waving the Law, and betrothing himselfe to no art or profession, that might justly denominate him, he began to survey the body of Divinity, controverted between the Reformed and Roman Church. And *as Gods blessed Spirit did then awaken him to the search, and in that industry did never forsake him*, (they be his owne words) *So be calls the same Spirit to witness to his Protestation, that in that search and disquisition he proceeded with humility and diffidence in himselfe, by the safest way of frequent Prayers, and indifferent affection to both parties.*[1] And indeed, Truth had too much
20 light about her, to be hid from so sharp an Inquirer, and he had too much ingenuity, not to acknowledge he had seen her.

Being to undertake this search, he beleeved the learned Cardinal *Bellarmine* to be the best defender of the Roman cause: and therefore undertook the examination of his reasons. The cause was waighty, and wilfull delaies had been inexcusable towards God and his own conscience; he therefore proceeded with all moderate haste; And before he entered into the twentieth yeare of his age, did shew the
30 Deane of Gloucester all the Cardinalls Works marked with many waighty Observations under his own hand, which Works were bequeathed by him at his death as a Legacy to a most deare friend.

[1] Preface to *Pseudo-Martyr*.

About the twentieth yeare of his age, he resolved to travell;
And the Earle of Essex going to Cales, and after the Iland
voyages, he took the advantage of those opportunities,
waited upon his Lordship, and saw the expeditions of those
happy and unhappy imployments.

But he returned not into England, till he had staid a convenient time, first in *Italy*, and then in *Spaine*, where he
made many usefull Observations of those Countries, their
Lawes, and Government, and returned into England perfect
in their Languages.   10

Not long after his returne, that exemplary pattern of
gravity and wisdome, the Lord *Elsmore*, Lord Keeper of the
great Seale, and after Chancellor of England, taking notice
of his Learning, Languages, and other abilities, and much
affecting both his person and condition, received him to be
his chiefe Secretarie, supposing it might be an Introduction
to some more waighty imployment in the State, for which
his Lordship often protested he thought him very fit.

Nor did his Lordship account him so much to be his servant, as to forget hee had beene his friend; and to testifie it, 20
hee used him alwayes with much curtesie, appointing him a
place at his owne Table, unto which he esteemed his company
and discourse a great ornament.

He continued that employment with much love and approbation, being daily usefull (and not mercenary) to his friends,
for the space of five yeares: In which time, he (I dare not say
unfortunately) fell into such a liking, as (with her approbation) increased into a love with a young Gentlewoman, who
lived in that Family, Neece to the Lady *Elsmore*, Daughter
to Sir *George More*, Chancellor of the Garter, and Lieutenant 30
of the Tower.

Sir *George* had some intimation of their increasing love,
and the better to prevent it, did remove his Daughter to his
owne house, but too late, by reason of some faithful promises

interchangeably past, and inviolably to be kept between them.

Their love (a passion, which of all other Mankind is least able to command, and wherein most errors are committed) was in them so powerfull, that they resolved, and did marry without the approbation of those friends that might justly claime an interest in the advising and disposing of them.

Being married, the newes was (in favour to M. *Donne*, and with his allowance) by the Right Honourable *Henry* then
10 Earle of Northumberland, secretly and certainly intimated to Sir *George More*, to whom it was so immeasurably unwelcome, that (as though his passion of anger and inconsideration should exceed theirs of love and error) he ingaged his sister the Lady *Elsmore* to joyn with him to procure her Lord to discharge M. *Donne* the place he held under his Lordship. And although Sir *George* were remembred that Errors might be over-punisht, and therefore was desired to forbeare, till second considerations had cleered some scruples, yet he was restlesse untill his suit was granted, and the
20 punishment executed; The Lord Chancellor then (at M. *Donnes* dismission) protesting, he thought him a Secretary fitter for a King then a Subject.

But this physick of M. *Donnes* dismission was not strong enough to purge out all Sir *George* his choler, who was not satisfied, till M. *Donne*, and his Compupill in Cambridge that married him, M. *Samuel Brooke*, (who was after D. in D. and Master of Trinity Colledge in that University) and his brother M. *Christopher Brook* of Lincolns Inne, (who gave M. *Donne* his Wife, and witnessed the Mariage) were all
30 committed to severall Prisons.

M. *Donne* was first inlarged, who neither gave rest to his body, his braine, nor any friend, in whom he might hope to have any interest, untill he had procured the inlargement of his two imprisoned friends.

He was now at liberty, but his dayes were still cloudie, and being past this trouble, others did still multiply, for his Wife (to her extreame sorrow) was detained from him. And though with *Iacob*,[1] he endured not a hard service for her, yet he lost a good one, and was forced to get possession of her by a long suit in Law, which proved very chargeable, and more troublesome.

It was not long, but that Time and M. *Donnes* behaviour (which when it would intice, had a strange kind of irresistible art) had so dispassioned his Father in Law, That as the world had approved his Daughters choice, so he also could not choose but see a more then ordinary merit in his new Sonne, which melted him into so much remorse, that he secretly laboured his sons restauration into his place, using his owne, and his sisters power, but with no successe; The Lord Chancellor replying, That although he was unfainedly sorry for what he had done, yet it stood not with his credit to discharge and re-admit servants, at the request of passionate Petitioners.

Within a short time, Sir *George* appeared to be so far reconciled, as to wish their happinesse; (or say so) And being asked for his paternal blessing, did not deny it; but refused to contribute any meanes that might conduce to their livelyhood.

M. *Donnes* Portion was the greatest part spent in many and chargeable travels, the rest disburst in some few Books, and deare bought experience; he out of all imployment, that might yeeld a support for himselfe and Wife, who had been curiously and plentifully educated; his nature generous, and he accustomed to confer, not to receive curtesies. These and other considerations, but chiefly that his deare Wife was to bear a part in his sufferings, surrounded him with many and sad thoughts, and some apparent apprehensions of want.

[1] Genes. 29.

But his sorrow was lessened, and his wants prevented by the seasonable curtesies of their noble Kinsman Sir *Francis Wally* of *Pirford*, who intreated them to a co-habitation with him; where they remained with very much freedome to themselves, and equall content to him for many yeares. And as their charge increased, (she had yearly a child) so did his love and bounty.

With him they continued till his death: a little before which time Sir *Francis* was so happy as to make a perfect
10 reconciliation betwixt that good man Sir *George More* and his forsaken sonne and daughter, Sir *George* then giving Bond to pay M. *Donne* 800 l. at a certain day as a Portion with his wife, and to pay him for their maintenance 20. l. quarterly, (as the Interest of it) untill the said Portion were paid.

Most of those yeares that he lived with Sir *Francis*, he studied the Civil and Canon Lawes: In which he acquired such a perfection as was judged to hold some proportion with many, who had made that study the imployment of their whole life.

20 Sir *Francis* being dead, and that happy family dissolved, M. *Donne* took a house at Micham (neere unto Croydon in Surrey) where his wife and family remained constantly: and for himselfe (having occasions to be often in London) he tooke lodgings neere unto White-hall, where he was frequently visited by men of greatest learning and judgement in this Kingdome; his company being loved, and much desired by many of the Nobility of this Nation, who used him in their counsels of greatest considerations.

Nor did our owne Nobility onely favour him, but his
30 acquaintance and friendship was usually sought for by most Ambassadors of forraigne Nations, and by many other strangers, whose learning or employment occasioned their stay in this Kingdome.

He was much importuned by friends to make his residence

in London, which he could not doe, having setled his dear
wife and children at Micham, whither he often retired himselfe, and then studied incessantly some Points of Con-
troversie. But at last the perswasion of friends was so
powerfull, as to cause the removall of himselfe and family to
London ; where that honourable Gentleman Sir *Robert Drury*
assigned him a very convenient house rent-free, next his own
in Drury-lane, and was also a daily cherisher of his studies,
and such a friend as sympathiz'd with him and his, in their
joy and sorrow.   10

Divers of the Nobility were watchfull and solicitous to the
King for some preferment for him. His Majesty had formerly
both knowne, and much valued him, and had given him some
hopes of a State employment, being much pleased that M.
Donne attended him, especially at his meales, where there
was usually many deep discourses of Learning, and often
friendly disputes of Religion betwixt the King and those
Divines whose places required their attendance on his
Majestie: Particularly, the Right Reverend Bishop *Monta-*
gue, then Deane of the Chappel, (who was the publisher of 20
the eloquent and learned Works of his Majestie) and the
most learned Doctor *Andrewes,* then his Majesties Almoner,
and at his death Bishop of Winchester.

About this time grew many disputes in England, that concerned the Oath of Supremacy and Allegeance, in which the
King had appeared and ingaged himselfe by his publique
writings now extant. And his Majestie occasionally talking
with M. *Donne* concerning many of those Arguments urged by
the Romanists, apprehended such a validity and cleerenesse
in his answers, that he commanded him to state the Points, 30
and bring his Reasons to him in writing; to which he
presently applyed himselfe, and within six weeks brought
them to his Majestie fairely written under his owne hand,
as they be now printed in his *Pseudo-Martyr.*

When the King had read and considered that Book, he perswaded M. *Donne* to enter into the Ministery, to which he appeared (and was) un-inclinable, apprehending it (such was his mistaking modesty) too weighty for his abilities. But from that time, though many friends mediated with his Majestie to prefer him to some civil employment, (to which his education had apted him) yet the King denied their requests, and (having a discerning spirit) replyed, *I know M. Donne is a learned man, an excellent Divine, and will* 10 *prove a powerfull Preacher.* After that, as he professeth,[1] the King descended almost to a solicitation of him to enter into sacred Orders, which though he denied not, he deferred for the space of three yeares: All which time he applyed himselfe to an incessant study of Textuall Divinity, and attained a greater perfection in the learned Languages, Greek and Hebrew.

Forwardnesse and inconsideration could not in him (as in many others) argue an insufficiencie; for he considered long, and had many strifes within himselfe concerning the strict-
20 nesse of life, and competencie of learning required in such as enter into sacred Orders: And doubtlesse (considering his owne demerits) did with meek *Moses* humbly aske God, *Who am I?* And if he had consulted with flesh and bloud, he had not put his hand to that holy plough: But God who is able to prevaile, wrastled with him, as the Angel did with *Iacob*,[2] and marked him for his owne, marked him with a blessing, a blessing of obedience to the motions of his blessed Spirit; And then as he had formerly asked God humbly with *Moses*, *Who am I?* So now (being inspired with the appre-
30 hension of Gods mercies) he did ask King *Davids* thankfull question, *Lord who am I that thou art so mindfull of me?* So mindfull of me as to lead me for more then forty years through a wildernesse of the many temptations and various

[1] In his Devotions, Expost. 8.   [2] Gen. 32.

turnings of a dangerous life? So mindfull as to move the learnedst of Kings to descend to move me to serve at thine Altar? So merciful to me as to move my heart to embrace this holy motion? Thy motions I will embrace, take the cup of salvation, call upon thy Name, and preach thy Gospell.

Such strifes as these S. *Augustine* had when S. *Ambrose* indeavoured his conversion to Christianity, with which he confesseth he acquainted his deare friend *Alippius*. Our learned Author (a man fit to write after no meane Copy) did the like; and declaring his intentions to his deare friend 10 D. *King* the then worthy Bishop of London, (who was Chaplaine to the Lord Chancellor in the time of his being his Lordships Secretary) That Reverend Bishop most gladly received the newes, and with all convenient speed ordained him Deacon and Priest.

Now the English Church had gained a second S. *Augustine,* for I think none was so like him before his conversion, none so like S. *Ambrose* after it. And if his youth had the infirmities of the one Father, his age had the excellencies of the other, the learning and holinesse of both.   20

Now all his studies (which were occasionally diffused) were concentred in Divinity; Now he had a new calling, new thoughts, new imployment for his wit and eloquence. Now all his earthly affections were changed into divine love, and all the faculties of his soule were ingaged in the conversion of others, in preaching glad tidings, remission to repenting sinners, and peace to each troubled soule: To this he applyed himselfe with all care and diligence; and such a change was wrought in him, that he was *gladder to be a doore-keeper in the house of God, then to enjoy any temporall* 30 *employment.*[1]

Presently after he entred into his holy Profession, the King made him his Chaplaine in Ordinary, and gave him

[1] Psal. 84.

other incouragements, promising to take a particular care
of him.

And though his long familiarity with persons of greatest
quality was such as might have given some men boldnesse
enough to have preached to any eminent Auditory; yet his
modesty was such, that he could not be perswaded to it, but
went usually to preach in some private Churches, in Villages
neere London, till his Majestie appointed him a day to
preach to him. And though his Majestie and others expected
10 much from him, yet he was so happy (which few are) as to
satisfie and exceed their expectations: preaching the Word
so, as shewed he was possest with those joyes that he laboured
to distill into others: A Preacher in earnest, weeping sometimes for his Auditory, sometimes with them, alwayes
preaching to himselfe, like an Angel from a cloud, though
in none: carrying some (as S. *Paul* was) to heaven, in holy
raptures; enticing others, by a sacred art and courtship, to
amend their lives; and all this with a most particular grace,
and un-imitable fashion of speaking.

20   That Summer, the same month in which he was ordained
Priest, (and made the Kings Chaplaine) his Majestie (going
his Progresse) was intreated to receive an entertainment in
the University of Cambridge, and M. *Donne* attending his
Majestie there, his Majestie was pleased to recommend him
to be made Doctor in Divinity, Doctor *Harsnet* (after Archbishop of York) being then their Vice-Chancellour, who
knowing him to be the Author of the *Pseudo-Martyr*, did
propose it to the University, and they presently granted it,
expressing a gladnesse they had an occasion to entitle and
30 write him Theirs.

His abilities and industry in his profession were so eminent,
and he so much loved by many persons of quality, that within
one yeare after his entrance into Sacred Orders, he had fourteen Advowsons of severall Benefices sent unto him; but

they (being in the Countrey) could not draw him from his long loved friends and London, to which he had a naturall inclination, having received his birth and breeding in it: desiring rather some preferment that might fixe him to an employment in that place.

Immediately after his returne from Cambridge, his wife died, leaving him a man of an unsetled estate: And (having buried five) the carefull father of seven children then living, to whom he made a voluntary promise (being then but forty two years of age) never to bring them under the subjection of a 10 Step-mother: which promise he most faithfully kept, burying with his teares all his sublunary joyes in his most deare and deserving Wives grave, living a most retired and solitary life.

In his retirednesse, he was importuned by the grave Benchers of Lincolns Inne, (once the friends of his youth) to accept of their Lecture, which (by reason of M. *Gatakers* removall) was then void; of which he accepted, being glad to renew his intermitted friendship with them, whom he so much loved, and where he had been a *Saul*, (not so far as to persecute Christianity, yet in his irregular youth to neglect 20 the practise of it) to become a *Paul*, and preach salvation to his brethren.

Nor did he preach onely, but as S. *Paul* advised his *Corinthians* to be followers of him as he was of Christ; so he also was an ocular direction to them by a holy and harmlesse conversation.

Their love to him was exprest many wayes; for (besides the faire lodgings that were provided and furnisht for him) other curtesies were daily accumulated, so many, and so freely, as though they meant their gratitude (if possible) 30 should exceed, or at least equall his merit. In this love-strife of desert and liberality, they continued for the space of three yeares; he constantly and faithfully preaching, they liberally requiting him. About which time the Emperour of *Germany* died, and the Palsgrave was elected and crowned King of Bohemia, the unhappy beginning of much trouble in those Kingdomes.

King *Iames*, whose Motto, *Beati Pacifici*, did truly characterize his disposition, endeavoured to compose the differences of that discomposed State, and to that end sent the Earle of Carlile, (then Vicount Doncaster) his Ambassadour to those unsetled Princes, and (by a speciall command from his Majestie) D. *Donne* was appointed to attend the
10 Embassage of the said Earle to the Prince of the Union: For which the Earle (that had long knowne and loved him) was most glad: So were many of the Doctors friends, who feared his studies, and sadnesse for his wives death, would as *Iacob* sayes, *make his dayes few*, and (respecting his bodily health) *evill too.*[1]

At his going, he left his friends of Lincolnes Inne, and they him with many reluctations; For though he could not say, as S. *Paul* to his Ephesians, *Behold, you to whom I have preacht the kingdome of God, shall henceforth see my face no more*; yet
20 he (being in a Consumption) questioned it, and they feared it, considering his troubled minde, which, with the helpe of his un-intermitted studies, hastned the decayes of his weake body; But God turned it to the best, for this imployment did not onely divert him from those serious studies and sad thoughts, but gave him a new and true occasion of joy, to be an eye-witnesse of the health of his honoured Mistris, the Queene of Bohemia, in a forraigne Land, (who having formerly knowne him a Courtier) was most glad to see him in a Canonicall habit, and more glad to be an eare-witnesse
30 of his most excellent and powerfull preaching.

Within fourteen moneths he returned to his friends of Lincolnes Inne, with his sorrowes much moderated, and his health improved.

[1] Gen. 47.

About a yeare after his returne from Germany, Dr. *Cary*
was made Bishop of Exeter, and by his removall, the
Deanry of S. *Pauls* being vacant, the King appointed Doctor
Donne to waite on him at dinner the next day; And his
Majesty (being set downe) before he eat any meat, said
(after his pleasant manner) *Doctor Donne, I have invited you
to dinner, And though you sit not downe with me, yet I will
carve to you of a dish that I know you love; you love London
well, I doe therefore make you Deane of Pauls, take your
meate home to your study, say grace, and much good may it* 10
doe you.

Immediately after he came to his Deanry, he imployed
workmen to repaire the Chappel belonging to his house;
Suffering (as holy *David* once vowed) *his eyes and temples to
take no rest, untill he had first beautified the house of God.*[1]

The next quarter following, when his Father in Law Sir
George More, who now admired and dearly loved him, came
to pay him the conditioned sum of twenty pound, he denied
to receive it, And said to his Father, (as good *Iacob* said when
he heard *Ioseph* his sonne lived) *It is enough,*[2] you have been 20
kinde to me, and carefull of mine, I am, I thanke my God,
provided for, and will receive this money no longer; And
not long after freely gave up his bond of eight hundred
pound.

Presently after he was setled in his Deanry, the Vicarage
of S. Dunstans in London fell to him by the death of Doctor
White, The advowson being formerly given to him by the
right Honorable *Richard* Earle of Dorset a little before his
death, And confirmed to him by his Brother the right
Honorable *Edward* Earle of Dorset that now lives. 30

By these and another Ecclesiasticall Endowment (which
fell to him about the same time) he was inabled to be
charitable to the poore, and to make such provision for his

[1] Psal. 132.   [2] Gen. 45.

Children, that at his death they were not left scandalous to his profession and quality.

The next Parliament following he was chosen Prolocutor to the Convocation, and about that time, by the appointment of his Majesty, (his gracious Master) did preach many occasionall Sermons: All which he performed not onely with the approbation, but to the admiration of the representative body of the Clergy of this Kingdome.

He was once (and but once) clouded with the Kings dis-
10 pleasure; It was about this time, occasioned by some malicious whisperer, which assured the King Doctor *Donne* had preacht a Sermon that implied a dislike of his government, particularly of his late Directions that the Evening Lectures on Sundaies, should be turned into Catechizing, expounding the Commandements, Beliefe, and Lords Prayer. His Majesty was the more inclinable to beleeve this, for that about the same time a person of the Nobility of great note in the Kingdome, and favour with the King (whom his Majesty knew Doctor *Donne* loved very much) was discarded
20 the Court, and presently after committed to prison, which begot many rumors in the multitude.

The King suffered not the Sunne to set, till he had searcht out the truth of this report, but sent presently for Doctor *Donne*, and required his answer to the accusation: which was so satisfactory, That the King said he was glad he rested not under that suspition. Doctor *Donne* protested his answer was faithfull and free from all Collusion. And therefore begged of his Majesty, that he might not rise (being then kneeling) before he had (as in like cases he alwayes had from
30 God) some assurance that he stood cleere and faire in his Majesties opinion. The King with his own hand, did, or offered to raise him from his knees, and protested he was truly satisfied, that he was an honest man, and loved him. Presently his Majesty called some Lords of his Councell into

his Chamber, and said with much earnestnesse, *My Doctor is an honest man*; And my Lords, I was never more joyed in anything that I have done, then in making him a Divine.

He was made Deane in the fiftieth yeare of his age; And in the fifty fourth yeare, a dangerous sicknesse seised him, which turned to a spotted Feaver, and ended in a Cough, that inclined him to a Consumption. But God (as *Iob* thankfully acknowledgeth) preserved his spirit, keeping his intellectualls as cleere and perfect, as when that sicknesse first seised his body. And as his health increased, so did his thankfulnesse, testified in his booke of Devotions, A book that may not unfitly be called, *A composition of holy Extasies*, occasioned, and appliable to the Emergencies of that sicknesse, which booke (being Meditations in his sicknesse) he writ on his sicke bed; herein imitating the holy Patriarchs, who were wont in that place to build their Altars where they had received their blessing.[1]

This sicknesse brought him to the gates of death, and he saw the grave so ready to devoure him, that he calls his recovery supernaturall. But God restored his health, and continued it untill the fifty-ninth yeare of his life. And then in August 1630. being with his daughter Mistris *Harvy* at Abrey-Hatch in Essex, he fell into a Feaver, which with the helpe of his constant infirmity, *vapours from the spleene*, hastened him into so visible a Consumption, that his beholders might say (as S. *Paul* of himselfe) *he dyes daily*, And he might say with *Iob*, *My welfare passeth away as a cloud; The dayes of affliction have taken hold of me. And weary nights are appointed for me.*[2]

This sicknesse continued long, not onely weakning, but wearing him so much, that my desire is, he may now take some rest: And that thou judge it no impertinent digression (before I speake of his death) to looke backe with me upon

[1] Gen. 12. 7-8. Gen. 28. 18.   [2] Job 30. 15. Job 7. 3.

2179·36   C

some observations of his life, which (while a gentle slumber seises him) may (I hope fitly) exercise thy Consideration.

His marriage was the remarkable error of his life, which (though he had a wit apt enough, and very able to maintaine paradoxes; And though his wives competent yeares, and other reasons might be justly urged to moderate a severe censure; yet) he never seemed to justifie, and doubtlesse had repented it, if God had not blest them with a mutuall, and so cordiall an affection, as in the midst of their sufferings made their bread
10 of sorrow taste more pleasantly then the banquet of fooles.

The recreations of his youth were Poetry, in which he was so happy, as if nature with all her varieties had been made to exercise his great wit, and high fancy. And in those pieces which were carelesly scattered in his younger daies (most of them being written before the twentieth yeare of his age) it may appeare by his choice Metaphors, that all the Arts joyned to assist him with their utmost skill.

It is a truth, that in his penitentiall yeares, viewing some of those pieces loosely scattered in his youth, he wisht they
20 had been abortive, or so short-liv'd, that he had witnessed their funeralls: But though he was no friend to them, he was not so falne out with heavenly Poetry, as to forsake it, no not in his declining age, witnessed then by many divine Sonnets, and other high, holy, and harmonious composures; yea even on his former sick bed, he wrote this heavenly Hymne, expressing the great joy he then had in the assurance of Gods mercy to him.

A Hymne to God the Father.

WILT thou forgive that sin where I begun,
30   Which was my sin, though it were done before?
Wilt thou forgive that sin through which I run,
     And doe run still, though still I doe deplore?
     When thou hast done, thou hast not done,
          For I have more.

Wilt thou forgive that sin which I have won
  Others to sin, and made my sin their dore?
Wilt thou forgive that sin which I did shun
  A yeare or two, but wallowed in, a score?
    When thou hast done, thou hast not done,
      For I have more.

I have a sin of feare, that when I have spun
  My last thred, I shall perish on the shore;
But sweare by thy selfe, that at my death thy Sonne
  Shall shine as he shines now, and heretofore;   10
    And, having done that, thou hast done,
      I feare no more.

And on this (which was his Death-bed) writ another
Hymne which bears this Title,

A Hymne to God my God in my sicknesse.

If these fall under the censure of a soule whose too much
mixture with earth makes it unfit to judge of these high
illuminations, let him know, that many devout and learned
men have thought the soule of holy *Prudentius* was most
refined, when not many dayes before his death, he charged 20
it to present his God each morning with a new and spirituall
Song; justified by the examples of King *David*, and the good
King *Hezekias*, who upon the renovation of his yeares, payed
his gratefull vowes to God, in a royall hymne, which he con-
cludes in these words, *The Lord was ready to save, therefore
we will sing my songs to the stringed instruments, all the dayes
of our life, in the Temple of my God.*[1]

The later part of his life was a continued studie, Saturdaies
onely excepted, which he usually spent in visiting friends,
and resting himselfe under the weary burthen of his weeks 30
Meditations; And he gave himselfe this rest, that thereby
he might be refresht and inabled to doe the work of the day
following, not negligently, but with courage and cheerfulnesse.

[1] Esay 38.

Nor was his age onely so industrious, but in his most unsetled youth he was (being in health) never knowne to be in
bed after foure of the clock in the morning, nor usually out
of his chamber till ten; and imployed that time constantly
(if not more) in his Studie. Which, if it seeme strange, may
gain beliefe by the visible fruits of his labours: some of
which remaine to testifie what is here written: for he left
the resultance of 1400 Authors, most of them analyzed with
his owne hand; He left sixscore Sermons also, all writ with
10 his owne hand; A large and laborious Treatise concerning
Selfe-murther, called *Biathanatose*, wherein all the Lawes
violated by that act, are diligently survayed, and judiciously
censured; A Treatise written in his youth, which alone might
declare him then, not onely perfect in the Civil and Canon
Law, but in many other such studies and arguments as enter
not into the consideration of many profest Scholars, that
labour to be thought learned Clerks, and to know all things.

Nor were these onely found in his Studie, but all businesses
that past of any publique consequence in this or any of our
20 neighbour Kingdoms, he abbreviated either in Latine, or in
the Language of the Nation, and kept them by him for a
memoriall. So he did the Copies of divers Letters and Cases
of Conscience that had concerned his friends, (with his
solutions) and divers other businesses of importance, all
particularly and methodically digested by himselfe.

He did prepare to leave the world before life left him,
making his Will when no facultie of his soule was dampt or
defective by sicknesse, or he surprized by sudden apprehen-
sion of death; But with mature deliberation, expressing
30 himselfe an impartiall Father, by making his Childrens
Portions equall; a constant lover of his friends, by particular
Legacies, discreetly chosen, and fitly bequeathed them; And
full of charity to the poore, and many others, who by his long
continued bounty might entitle themselves *His almes-people*.

For all these he made provision, so largely, as having six
children, might to some appeare more then proportionable
to his estate. The Reader may think the particulars tedious,
but I hope not impertinent, that I present him with the
beginning and conclusion of his last Will.

In the name of the blessed and glorious Trinitie, Amen. I Iohn
Donne, by the mercy of Christ Iesus, and the calling of the
Church of England, Priest, being at this time in good and perfect understanding, (praised be God therefore) doe hereby make
my last Will and Testament in manner and forme following.   10
   First, I give my gracious God an intire sacrifice of body and
soule, with my most humble thanks for that assurance which
his blessed Spirit imprints in me now of the salvation of the one,
and of the resurrection of the other; And for that constant and
cheerfull resolution which the same Spirit established in me, to
live and die in the Religion now professed in the Church of
England: In expectation of that Resurrection I desire my body
may be buried (in the most private manner that may be) in that
place of S. *Pauls* Church London, that the now Residentiaries
have at my request assigned for that purpose, &c.   20
   And this my last Will and Testament made in the feare of
God, (whose merit I humbly beg, and constantly rely upon in
Iesus Christ) and in perfect love and charity with all the world,
whose pardon I aske from the lowest of my servants to the
highest of my Superiours. Written all with mine owne hand,
and my name subscribed to every Page, being five in number.

Nor was his charity exprest onely at his death, but in his
life, by a cheerfull and frequent visitation of friends, whose
minds were dejected, or fortunes necessitous. And he re-
deemed many out of Prison that lay for small debts, or for   30
their fees; He was a continuall giver to poore Scholars, both
of this, and forraigne Nations; (besides what he gave with
his owne hand) he usually sent a servant to all the Prisons in
London, to distribute his charity, at all festivall times in the
yeare. He gave 100. l. at one time to a Gentleman that he
had formerly knowne live plentifully, and was then decayed

in his estate. He was a happy Reconciler of differences in many Families of his friends and kindred, who had such faith in his judgement and impartiality, that he scarce ever advised them to any thing in vaine. He was (even to her death) a most dutifull son to his Mother, carefull to provide for her supportation, of which she had been destitute, but that God raised him up to prevent her necessities; who having suckt in the Religion of the Romane Church with her mothers milk, (or presently after it) spent her estate in
10 forraigne Countries, to enjoy a liberty in it, and died in his house but three moneths before him.

And to the end it may appeare how just a Steward he was of his Lord and Masters Revenue, I have thought fit to let the Reader know, that after his entrance into his Deanry, as he numbred his yeares, and (at the foot of a private account, to which God and Angels onely were witnesses with him) computed first his Revenue, then his expences, then what was given to the poore and pious uses, lastly, what rested for him and for his, he blest each yeares poore
20 remainder with a thankfull Prayer; which for that they discover a more then common devotion, the Reader shall partake some of them in his owne words.

1624.   So all is that remains ⎫
1625.   of these two years ⎭

Deo Opt. Max. benigno Largitori, à me, & ab iis quibus haec à me reservantur, gloria, & gratia in æternum. Amen.
1626.   So that this yeare God hath blessed ⎫
                    me and mine with   ⎭

Multiplicatæ sunt super nos misericordiæ tuæ Domine.
30 *Da Domine, ut quæ ex immensa bonitate tua nobis elargiri dignatus sis, in quorumcunque manus devenerint, in tuam semper cedant gloriam. Amen.*

1628.   *In fine horum sex annorum manet*

1629.

Quid habeo, quod non accepi à Domino? Largiatur etiam, ut quæ largitus est, sua iterum fiant bono eorum usu, ut quemadmodum, nec officiis hujus mundi, nec loci, in quo me posuit, dignitati, nec servis, nec egenis, in toto hujus anni curriculo, mihi conscius sum, me defuisse, ita [ut] liberi, quibus quæ supersunt, supersunt, grato animo ea accipiant, & beneficum Authorem recognoscant. Amen.

But I returne from my digression.

We left the Author sick in Essex, where he was forced to 10 spend most of that Winter, by reason of his disability to remove from thence. And having never during almost twenty yeares, omitted his personall attendance on his Majestie, in his monthly service. Nor being ever left out of the number of Lent Preachers. And in January following, there being a generall report that he was dead, that report occasioned this Letter to a familiar friend.

SIR,
This advantage you and my other friends have by my frequent feavers, that I am so much the oftner at the gates of heaven; 20 And this advantage by the solitude and close imprisonment that they reduce me to after, that I am so much the oftner at my Prayers, in which I shall never leave out your happinesse; And I doubt not but amongst his other blessings, God will adde some one to you for my Prayers.

A man would be almost content to die, (if there were no other benefit in death) to heare of so much sorrow, and so much good testimony from good men, as I (God be blessed for it) did upon the report of my death: Yet I perceive it went not through all; For one writ to me, that some (and he said of my friends) con- 30 ceived I was not so ill as I pretended, but withdrew my selfe to live at ease, discharged of preaching. It is an unfriendly, and (God knowes) an ungrounded interpretation; for I have alwayes been sorrier when I could not preach, then any could be they could not hear me. It hath been my desire (and God may be pleased to grant it) that I might die in the Pulpit; If not that, yet that I might take my death in the Pulpit, that is, die the

sooner by occasion of those labours. Sir, I hope to see you presently after Candlemas, about which time will fall my Lent
Sermon at Court, except my Lord Chamberlaine beleeve me to
be dead, and leave me out: For as long as I live, and am not
speechlesse, I would not willingly decline that service. I have
better leasure to write, then you to reade, yet I would not
willingly oppresse you with too much Letter: God blesse you
and your son, as I wish

      January 7.   Your poore friend and servant
10   1630.   in Christ Jesus,
                                  Iohn Donne.

    Before that month ended, he was appointed to preach
upon his old constant day, the first Friday in Lent, he had
notice of it; and having in his sicknesse prepared for the
employment as he had long thirsted for it. So resolving his
weaknesse should not hinder his journey, he came to London
some few dayes before his day appointed. Being come,
many of his friends (who with sorrow saw his sicknesse had
left him onely so much flesh as did cover his bones) doubted
20 his strength to performe that taske: And therefore perswaded
him from undertaking it, assuring him however, it was like
to shorten his dayes: But he passionately denyed their requests, saying, He would not doubt, that God who in many
weaknesses had assisted him with an unexpected strength,
would ⟨not⟩ now withdraw it in his last employment,
professing a holy ambition to performe that sacred Work.
And when (to the amazement of some beholders) he appeared
in the Pulpit, many thought he presented himselfe, not to
preach mortification by a living voice, but mortality by a
30 decayed body, and dying face. And doubtlesse many did
secretly ask that question in *Ezekiel, Doe these bones live?*[1]
Or can that soule organise that tongue to speak so long time
as the sand in that glasse will move towards its center, and
measure out an houre of this dying mans unspent life?

                  [1] Ezek. 37. **3.**

Doubtlesse it cannot. Yet after some faint pauses in his zealous Prayer, his strong desires inabled his weak body to discharge his memory of his pre-conceived Meditations which were of dying; The Text being, *To God the Lord belong the issues from death.* Many that saw his teares, and heard his hollow voice, professing they thought the Text Prophetically chosen, and that D. *Donne* had preacht his owne Funerall Sermon.

Being full of joy that God had inabled him to performe this desired duty, he hastned to his house, out of which he never moved, untill like S. *Stephen, He was carried by devout men to his grave:*[1] And the next day after his Sermon, his spirits being much spent, and he indisposed to discourse, a friend asked him, Why are you sad? To whom he replyed after this manner, 'I am not sad; I am in a serious contemplation of the mercies of my God to me; And now I plainly see, it was his hand that prevented me from all temporall employment. And I see it was his will that I should never settle nor thrive untill I entred into the Ministery, in which I have now lived almost twenty yeares, (I hope to his glory) and by which (I most humbly thank him) I have been enabled to requite most of those friends that shewed me kindnesse when my fortunes were low. And (as it hath occasioned the expression of my gratitude) I thank God, most of them have stood in need of my requitall. I have been usefull and comfortable to my good Father in Law Sir *George More*, whose patience God hath been pleased to exercise by many temporall crosses. I have maintained my owne Mother, whom it hath pleased God after a plentifull fortune in her former times, to bring to a great decay in her very old age. I have quieted the consciences of many that groaned under the burthen of a wounded spirit, whose Prayers I hope are availeable for me. I cannot plead innocencie of

[1] Acts 8.

life, (especially of my youth) but I am to be judged by a mercifull God, who hath given me (even at this time) some testimonies by his holy Spirit, that I am of the number of his Elect. I am ful of joy, and shall die in peace.

Upon Munday following, he took his last leave of his beloved Studie, and being hourely sensible of his decay, retired himselfe into his bed-chamber: and that week sent (at severall times) for many of his most considerable friends, of whom he tooke a solemne and deliberate Farewell, com-
10 mending to their considerations some sentences particularly usefull for the regulation of their lives, and dismist them (as *Iacob*[1] did his sons) with a spirituall benediction. The Sunday following, he appointed his servants, that if there were any worldly businesse undone, that concerned them or himselfe, it should be prepared against Saturday next; for after that day he would not mixe his thoughts with any thing that concerned the world. Nor ever did.

Now he had nothing to doe but die; To doe which, he stood in need of no more time, for he had long studied it,
20 and to such a perfection, that in a former sicknesse he called God to witnesse,[2] he was that minute prepared to deliver his soule into his hands, if that minute God would accept of his dissolution. In that sickneese he begged of his God, (the God of constancy) to be preserved in that estate for ever. And his patient expectation to have his immortall soule disrobed from her garment of mortality, makes me confident he now had a modest assurance, that his prayers were then heard, and his petition granted. He lay fifteene dayes earnestly expecting his hourely change; And in the
30 last houre of his last day, (as his body melted away, and vapoured into spirit) his soule having (I verily beleeve) some revelation of the Beatifical Vision, he said, *I were miserable, if I might not die*: And after those words, closed many periods

[1] Gen. 49.   [2] Devot. Prayer 23.

of his faint breath with these words, *Thy Kingdome come,
Thy will be done.* His speech which had long been his faithfull servant, remained with him till his last minute; and
then forsook him, not to serve another master, but died
before him, for that it was uselesse to him, who now con-
versed with God on earth, (as Angels are said to doe in
heaven) onely by thoughts and looks. Being speechlesse, he
did (as S. *Stephen*) *look stedfastly towards heaven,* till he saw
the Sonne of God standing at the right hand of his Father;
And being satisfied with this blessed sight, (as his soule 10
ascended, and his last breath departed from him) he closed
his owne eyes, and then disposed his hands and body into
such a posture, as required no alteration by those that came
to shroud him.

Thus *variable,* thus *vertuous* was the *life,* thus *memor-
able,* thus *exemplary* was the *death* of this most excellent
man.

He was buried in S. *Pauls* Church, in that place which he
had appointed for that use, some yeares before his death,
and by which he passed daily to his devotions. But not 20
buried privately, though he desired it; For (besides an un-
numbred number of others) many persons of Nobility and
eminency, who did love and honour him in his life, did shew
it at his Funerall, by a voluntary and very sad attendance
of his body to the grave.

To which (after his buriall) some mournfull friends re-
paired: And as *Alexander* the Great did to the grave of the
famous *Achillis,*[1] so they strewed his with curious and costly
flowers. Which course they (who were never yet knowne)
continued each morning and evening for divers dayes, not 30
ceasing till the stones that were taken up in that Church to
give his body admission into the cold earth, (now his bed of
rest) were againe by the Masons art levelled and firmed, as

---

[1] Plutarch.

they had been formerly, and his place of buriall undistinguishable to common view.

Nor was this (though not usuall) all the honour done to his reverend ashes; for by some good body, (who, tis like thought his memory ought to be perpetuated) there was 100. marks sent to his two faithfull friends[1] and Executors, (the person that sent it, not yet known, they look not for a reward on earth) towards the making of a Monument for him, which I think is as lively a representation, as in dead
10 marble can be made of him.

HE was of stature moderately tall; of a straight and equally proportioned body, to which all his words and actions gave an unexpressible addition of comelinesse.

His aspect was cheerfull, and such as gave a silent testimony of a cleere knowing soule, and of a conscience at peace with it selfe.

His melting eye shewed he had a soft heart, full of noble pity, of too brave a spirit to offer injuries, and too much a Christian, not to pardon them in others.

20   His fancie was un-imitable high, equalled by his great wit, both being made usefull by a commanding judgement.

His mind was liberall, and unwearied in the search of knowledge, with which his vigorous soule is now satisfied, and employed in a continuall praise of that God that first breathed it into his active body, which once was a Temple of the holy Ghost, and is now become a small quantity of Christian dust. But I shall see it re-inanimated.

Iz: WA:

BEN JONSON ON DONNE

From *Notes of Ben Jonson's Conversations with William Drummond of Hawthornden*, 1619, first printed 1711

THAT Dones Anniversarie was profane and full of Blasphe-
30 mies.

That he told Mr Donne, if it had been written of the Virgin

[1] D. *Henry King.* D. *Mountfort.*

Marie it had been something, to which he answered that he
described the Idea of a Woman and not as she was.

That Done for not keeping of accent deserved hanging.

He esteemeth John Done the first poet in the world in some
things; his verses of the Lost Chaine he hath by Heart and
that passage of the calme, that dust and fethers do not stir,
all was so quiet.

Affirmeth Done to have written all his best pieces ere he
was 25 years old.

That Done himself for not being understood would perish. 10

DRUMMOND OF HAWTHORNDEN ON DONNE
From *Notes of Ben Jonson's Conversations with William Drummond
of Hawthornden*

DONNE, among the Anacreontick Lyricks, is Second to
none, and far from all Second. But as Anacreon doth not
approach *Callimachus*, tho' he excels in his own kind, nor
Horace to *Virgil*, no more can I be brought to think him to
excel either *Alexander's* or *Sidney's* Verses. They can hardly
be compared together, trading diverse Paths,—the one flying
swift but low, the other, like the Eagle, surpassing the
Clouds. I think, if he would, he might easily be the best
Epigrammatist we have found in English, of which I have
not yet seen any come near the Ancients. 20

Compare Song, *Marry and Love*, &c., with *Tasso's Stanzas
against Beauty*; one shall hardly know who hath the best.

DRYDEN ON DONNE
(a) From *Of Dramatick Poesie, An Essay*, 1668

'TIS true, no poet but may sometimes use a *Catachresis* ...
But to do this alwayes, and never be able to write a line without it, though it may be admired by some few Pedants, will
not pass upon those who know that wit is best convey'd to
us in the most easie language; and is most to be admir'd

when a great thought comes drest in words so commonly
receiv'd, that it is understood by the meanest apprehensions, as the best meat is the most easily digested; but we
cannot read a verse of *Cleveland's* without making a face at
it, as if every word were a Pill to swallow; he gives us many
times a hard Nut to break our Teeth, without a Kernel for
our pains. So that there is this difference betwixt his *Satyres*
and doctor Donn's; That the one gives us deep thoughts in
common language, though rough cadence; the other gives
10 us common thoughts in abstruse words.

(b) From *The Original and Progress of Satire*, 1693
[*to the Earl of Dorset*]

DONN alone, of all our Countrymen, had your Talent; but
was not happy enough to arrive at your Versification; and
were he Translated into Numbers, and English, he wou'd yet
be wanting in the Dignity of Expression. ... You equal Donn
in the Variety, Multiplicity, and Choice of Thoughts; you
excel him in the Manner, and the Words. I Read you both
with the same Admiration, but not with the same Delight.
He affects the Metaphysicks, not only in his satires, but in
his Amorous Verses, where Nature only should reign; and
20 perplexes the Minds of the Fair Sex with nice Speculations
of Philosophy, when he shou'd ingage their Hearts, and
entertain them with the softnesses of Love. In this (if I may
be pardon'd for so bold a truth) Mr *Cowley* has Copy'd him
to a fault.

(c) Ibid.

WOU'D not Donn's *Satires*, which abound with so much Wit,
appear more Charming, if he had taken care of his Words,
and of his Numbers? But he followed *Horace* so very close,
that of necessity he must fall with him; and I may safely
say it of this present age, That if we are not so great Wits
30 as Donn, yet, certainly, we are better Poets.

ROBERT WOLSELEY ON DONNE
From the *Preface to Valentinian*, 1685

VERSES have Feet given 'em, either to walk graceful and smooth, and sometimes with Majesty and State, like Virgil's, or to run light and easie, like Ovid's, not to stand stock-still, like Dr Donne's, or to hobble like indigested Prose.

COLERIDGE ON DONNE
(*a*) From *Biographia Literaria*, 1817

ONE great distinction, I appeared to myself to see plainly, between, even, the characteristic faults of our elder poets, and the false beauty of the moderns. In the former, from DONNE to COWLEY, we find the most fantastic out-of-the-way thoughts, but in the most pure and genuine mother English; in the latter, the most obvious thoughts, in language 10 the most fantastic and arbitrary. Our faulty elder poets sacrificed the passion and passionate flow of poetry, to the subtleties of intellect, and to the starts of wit; the moderns to the glare and glitter of a perpetual, yet broken and heterogeneous imagery, or rather to an amphibious something, made up, half of image, and half of abstract meaning. The one sacrificed the heart to the head; the other both heart and head to point and drapery.

(*b*) From *Notes, Theological, Political, and Miscellaneous*, 1853

TO read Dryden, Pope, &c., you need only count syllables; but to read Donne you must measure *Time*, and discover the 20 *Time* of each word by the sense of Passion.

(*c*) From *Literary Remains*, 1836
i

With Donne, whose muse on dromedary trots,
Wreathe iron pokers into true-love knots;
Rhyme's sturdy cripple, fancy's maze and clue,
Wit's forge and fire-blast, meaning's press and screw.

ii

See lewdness and theology combined,—
A cynic and a sycophantic mind;
A fancy shared party per pale between
Death's heads and skeletons and Aretine!—
Not his peculiar defect or crime,
But the true current mintage of the time.
Such were the establish'd signs and tokens given
To mark a loyal churchman, sound and even,
Free from papistic and fanatic leaven.

10 The wit of Donne, the wit of Butler, the wit of Pope, the
wit of Congreve, the wit of Sheridan—how many disparate
things are here expressed by one and the same word, Wit!—
Wonder-exciting vigour, intenseness and peculiarity of
thought, using at will the almost boundless stores of a
capacious memory, and exercised on subjects where we
have no right to expect it—this is the wit of Donne!

LAMB ON DONNE
From *Mrs. Leicester's School, and Other Writings*, 1885, p. 358

DONNE and Cowley, by happening to possess more wit,
and faculty of illustration, than other men, are supposed to
have been incapable of nature or feeling; they are usually
20 opposed to such writers as Shenstone and Parnell; whereas,
in the very thickest of their conceits,—in the bewildering
mazes of tropes and figures,—a warmth of soul and generous
feeling shines through, the 'sum' of which 'forty thousand'
of those natural poets, as they are called, 'with all their
quantity', could not make up.

HAZLITT ON DONNE
From *The English Comic Writers*, 1819

THE writers here referred to (such as Donne, Davies,
Crashaw, and others) not merely mistook learning for
poetry—they thought anything was poetry that differed

from ordinary prose, and the natural impression of things,
by being intricate, far-fetched, and improbable. Their style
was not so properly learned as metaphysical; that is to say,
whenever, by any violence done to their ideas, they could
make out an abstract likeness or possible ground of comparison, they forced the image, whether learned or vulgar,
into the service of the Muses. . . . The imagination of the
writers, instead of being conversant with the face of nature,
or the secrets of the heart, was lost in the labyrinths of
intellectual abstraction, or entangled in the technical quib- 10
bles and impertinent intricacies of language. The complaint
so often made, and here repeated, is not of the want of power
in these men, but of the waste of it; not of the absence of
genius, but the abuse of it. They had (many of them) great
talents committed to their trust, richness of thought, and
depth of feeling; but they chose to hide them (as much as
they possibly could) under a false show of learning and
unmeaning subtlety. From the style which they had sys-
tematically adopted, they thought nothing done till they
had perverted simplicity into affectation, and spoiled nature 20
by art. . . . Their chief aim was to make you wonder at
the writer, not to interest you in the subject; and by an
incessant craving after admiration, they have lost what they
might have gained with less extravagance and affectation.
So Cowper, who was of a quite opposite school, speaks feelingly of the misapplication of Cowley's poetical genius.

> And though reclaim'd by modern lights
> From an erroneous taste,
> I cannot but lament thy splendid wit
> Entangled in the cobwebs of the schools.   30

Donne, who was considerably before Cowley, is without his
fancy, but was more recondite in his logic, and rigid in his
descriptions. He is hence led, particularly in his satires, to
tell disagreeable truths in as disagreeable a way as possible,

or to convey a pleasing and affecting thought (of which there
are many to be found in his other writings) by the harshest
means, and with the most painful effort. His Muse suffers
continual pangs and throes. His thoughts are delivered by
the Cæsarean operation. The sentiments, profound and
tender as they often are, are stifled in the expression; and
'heaved pantingly forth', are 'buried quick again' under
the ruins and rubbish of analytical distinctions. It is like
poetry waking from a trance: with an eye bent idly on the
10 outward world, and half-forgotten feelings crowding about
the heart; with vivid impressions, dim notions, and dis-
jointed words. The following may serve as instances of
beautiful or impassioned reflections losing themselves in
obscure and difficult applications. He has some lines to a
Blossom, which begin thus:

> Little think'st thou, poor flow'r,
> Whom I have watched six or seven days,
> And seen thy birth, and seen what every hour
> Gave to thy growth, thee to this height to raise,
20 And now dost laugh and triumph on this bough,
>   Little think'st thou
> That it will freeze anon, and that I shall
> To-morrow find thee fall'n, or not at all.

This simple and delicate description is only introduced as
a foundation for an elaborate metaphysical conceit as a
parallel to it, in the next stanza.

> Little think'st thou (poor heart
> That labour'st yet to nestle thee,
> And think'st by hovering here to get a part
30 In a forbidden or forbidding tree,
> And hop'st her stiffness by long siege to bow:)
>   Little think'st thou,
> That thou to-morrow, ere the sun doth wake,
> Must with this sun and me a journey take.

This is but a lame and impotent conclusion from so delight-

ful a beginning.—He thus notices the circumstance of his
wearing his late wife's hair about his arm, in a little poem
which is called the Funeral:

> Whoever comes to shroud me, do not harm
>   Nor question much
> That subtle wreath of hair, about mine arm;
> The mystery, the sign you must not touch.

The scholastic reason he gives quite dissolves the charm of
tender and touching grace in the sentiment itself—

>   For 'tis my outward soul,   10
> Viceroy to that, which unto heaven being gone,
>   Will leave this to control,
> And keep these limbs, her provinces, from dissolution.

Again, the following lines, the title of which is Love's Deity,
are highly characteristic of this author's manner, in which
the thoughts are inlaid in a costly but imperfect mosaic-
work:

> I long to talk with some old lover's ghost,
> Who died before the God of Love was born;
> I cannot think that he, who then lov'd most,   20
> Sunk so low, as to love one which did scorn.
> But since this God produc'd a destiny,
> And that vice-nature, custom, lets it be;
> I must love her that loves not me.

The stanza in the Epithalamion on a Count Palatine of the
Rhine has often been quoted against him, and is an almost
irresistible illustration of the extravagance to which this
kind of writing, which turns upon a pivot of words and
possible allusions, is liable. Speaking of the bride and bridegroom he says, by way of serious compliment—   30

> Here lies a she-Sun, and a he-Moon there,
> She gives the best light to his sphere;
> Or each is both and all, and so
> They unto one another nothing owe.

His love-verses and epistles to his friends give the most favourable idea of Donne. His satires are too clerical. He shows, if I may so speak, too much disgust, and, at the same time, too much contempt for vice. His dogmatical invectives hardly redeem the nauseousness of his descriptions, and compromise the imagination of his readers more than they assist their reason. The satirist does not write with the same authority as the divine, and should use his poetical privileges more sparingly. 'To the pure all things are pure', is a maxim which a man like Dr Donne may be justified in applying to himself; but he might have recollected that it could not be construed to extend to the generality of his readers, *without benefit of clergy*.

DE QUINCEY ON DONNE

From essay on 'Rhetoric', *Blackwood's Magazine*, December 1828

FEW writers have shown a more extraordinary compass of powers than Donne; for he combined what no other man has ever done—the last sublimation of dialectical subtlety and address with the most impassioned majesty. Massy diamonds compose the very substance of his poem on the Metempsychosis, thoughts and descriptions which have the fervent and gloomy sublimity of Ezekiel or Æschylus, whilst a diamond dust of rhetorical brilliancies is strewed over the whole of his occasional verses and his prose.

GEORGE SAINTSBURY ON DONNE

From *A Short History of English Literature*, 1898[1]

THE Songs exhibit Donne's quintessenced, melancholy, passionate imagination as applied, chiefly in youth, to Love; the Anniversaries, the same imagination as applied to

[1] By permission of Messrs. Macmillan & Co. Ltd.

Death, the ostensible text being the untimely death of
Mistress Elizabeth Drury, but the real subject being the
riddle of the painful earth as embodied in the death of the
body. The Songs are, of course, in different lyrical forms,
and the Anniversaries are in couplets. But both agree in
the unique *clangour* of their poetic sound, and in the extraordinary character of the thoughts which find utterance in
verse, now exquisitely melodious, now complicated and
contorted almost beyond ready comprehension in rhyme
or sense, but never really harsh, and always possessing, in 10
actual presence or near suggestion, a poetical quality which
no English poet has ever surpassed. It is from these poems
that the famous epithet 'metaphysical' (which Johnson not
too happily, and with a great confusion between Donne and
Cowley, applied to the whole school) is derived; and as
applied to Donne it is not inappropriate. For, behind every
image, every ostensible thought of his, there are vistas
and backgrounds of other thoughts dimly vanishing, with
glimmers in them here and there, into the depths of the
final enigmas of life and soul. Passion and meditation, the 20
two avenues into this region of doubt and dread, are tried
by Donne in the two sections respectively, and of each he
has the key. Nor, as he walks in them with eager or solemn
tread, are light and music wanting, the light the most un-
earthly that ever played round a poet's head, the music
not the least heavenly that he ever caught and transmitted
to his readers.

OLIVER ELTON ON DONNE
From *The English Muse*, 1933[1]

BUT already, about 1595, one young poet had broken with
the current styles; he refused to deal in smooth melodies,
in moral parables, in *translated* passions, or in 'poor Petrarch's 30

[1] By permission of Messrs. G. Bell & Sons, Ltd.

long-deceasèd woes'. He composed some highly acrid satires on contemporary manners; they are not poetry, and often, what with their wrenchings of the metrical accent, they are not verse. They were perhaps the earliest writings of John Donne (1573–1631), who was to rule, in the opinion of an admirer, 'the universal monarchy of wit'. The chief events in his outer life are his stolen marriage in 1601 with Anne More, followed by a spell of poverty and dependence; his conversion from the old faith, in which he was born; his
10 ordination in 1615 as a convinced Anglican and remorseful believer; the death of his wife in 1617; and his appointment in 1621 as Dean of St. Paul's. He died in 1631, the chief preacher of his time; his sermons outflame all others of the century. Most of his verse was posthumously published; the volumes of 1633 and 1635 are the most important. He also wrote much in prose, including *Devotions upon Emergent Occasions* (1624); *Biathanatos* (1648), a treatise to show that suicide is not always sinful; and certain *Paradoxes and Problems*: all of them showing, once more, that Donne was
20 a 'mental traveller' of the strangest complexion. The text and canon and dates and sequence of his poems, and often their interpretation, offer as many problems as the work of William Blake,—yet another genius who (like Shelley) makes all racial theories of the 'Anglo-Saxon' character look foolish.

The *Satires*, the *Elegies*, and some of those *Songs and Sonnets* which are Donne's best legacy, are thought to date from his bachelor days. It is clear that the harshness of his verse was wanton and deliberate; when he chooses, no one
30 can be more melodious, though the melodies are of a new order. For some of his songs, such as 'Go and catch a falling star', musical settings are known; but in general the mood shifts too suddenly, and the argument exacts too much thinking, for the rightful effect of a song. For beauty of

idea and execution, an anthologist might pick out 'Sweetest
Love'; the *Dream*; the *Anniversary*, with its wonderful
concerted rhythm, and its fancy that the lovers are *kings*,
keeping their state together; the *Sun Rising*, which opens
with Donne's favourite shock tactics ('Busy old fool, un-
ruly Sun'); and the *Canonization* ('For Godsake hold your
tongue, and let me love'). But every one of the fifty-five
Songs and Sonnets has its peculiar virtue. Many, and many
of the best, are frankly pagan, libertine, and unregenerate;
there is abundance of *odi et amo*, of *sentio et excrucior*. Yet 10
this strain is crossed, sometimes more and sometimes less,
by an idealistic one, with much harping on the Platonic
'union of souls'; and again, in the ebb of passion, by endless
subtle teasing of words and thoughts—the 'false wit' and
'conceits' on which Johnson falls so heavily. But even here
we have the impression of a fierce honesty. Not that these
poems help the biographer. It is not certainly known to
whom any of them are addressed; and we cannot say, nor
need we care, whether a particular piece records an actual
experience, or a dream wrought up from some fragment of 20
reality, or a pure imagination. Sometimes, as in *Break of
Day*, the speaker is a woman; it is the *aubade* of a Juliet
whose lover is perforce 'removed' from her by his business.
That splendid and brutal 'elegy', *On his Mistress* ('By our
first strange and fatal interview'), may or may not be as
purely dramatic as anything in Browning's *Men and Women*.
It is all highly *irritant* poetry, disquieted and disquieting;
its chief deficiency is that of any simple and direct feeling
for the beauty of the world. Even the beauty of women is
not seen simply; the restless refining intellect as it were 30
pounces on the vision and dissipates it in a thousand
reasonings.

Donne's vocabulary can be very pure and plain; it is close
to the natural prose, which is *staccato* and monosyllabic, of

love or anger. In the *Songs and Sonnets*, there are many
learned or scientific allusions, but not many unfamiliar terms.
Transubstantiate, interinanimate, are exceptional. The gram-
mar easily becomes elliptical and condensed; and, as a later
poet, Patrick Carey, observes: 'Words may be common,
clear, and pure, And yet the sense remain obscure.' Donne's
rhythmic movement, in consequence, is often hindered. He
must be read aloud slowly; much of his music comes from
those subtle doublings and shiftings of the stress, which, in
10 his favourite short lines, are all the more emphatic. He
asks, for instance, where a true and fair woman can be found:

> If thou find'st one, let me know,
>   Such a pilgrimage were sweet;
> Yet do not, I would not go,
>   Though at next door we might meet,
> Though she were true, when you met her,
> And last, till you write your letter,
>   Yet she
>   Will be
20 False, ere I come, to two, or three.

Much of the verse that is assigned to Donne's middle years
is merely repulsive to the artistic sense, in spite of some
(all too rare) blessed oases and glorious interludes. Such
are the soaring lines in the *Second Anniversary*:

> Think thou, my soul, that death is but a groom,
> Which brings a taper to the outward room . . .

with its conclusion, forestalling Donne's later mood:

> Only in Heaven joy's strength is never spent;
> And accidental things are permanent.

30 This is Donne's most transcendental long poem, and seems
to show some reading of Dante; it makes us long for Dante's
distinctness and superb sense of order. The *Letters, Epicedes*
and *Epitaphs* have the same kind of flaws and beauties
everywhere. But the *Progress of the Soul* is a Caliban of

a poem: the soul of man is traced from the apple of Eden through many horrid and fantastic incarnations; but, as in Caliban, there is music.

In Donne's prose letters and *Devotions* and sermons can be traced the slow painful shifting of his outlook from the things of earth to those of heaven. Some of the sacred pieces, the *Litany* and the *Annunciation and Passion* are dated about 1609, *La Corona* being also of this period; while two of the marriage songs, those on the Princess Elizabeth and on the Earl of Somerset, were written in 1613. 10 The first of these is the boldest and richest and strangest of its kind in English; it has more blood in it than Spenser's nobler ode. It is clear that the 'progress of the soul' in Donne was subject to secular backslidings, which it is impossible to regret. The *Divine Poems*, however, as a whole show his later frame of mind. They are not free from monotony, but they are alive with remorse and fear and expectancy and rapture; and, like his sermons, are sorely preoccupied with the physical aspects of death. Donne— to use a phrase which Robert Browning probably adapted 20 from him—is 'soul-hydroptic with a sacred thirst'. He does not attain the mystical vision properly so called; there are many glances backward, of repentance not unmixed with too keen a memory, at his wanton youth. He is seldom really at peace. Some of these poems come near to perfection. Such are the sonnets 'Death, be not proud, though some have called thee'; 'Thou hast made me, and shall thy work decay?'; and, above all, 'At the round earth's imagined corners blow', with its vision of the souls which at the Last Day 'shall to your scattered bodies go'. The 30 manner is the same as of old; the words are cut to the quick, the thought goes like a weaver's shuttle. But the imagination is now steadier and more consistently lofty, the execution less fitful. The erect and shrouded stone figure of the poet, to be seen in St. Paul's, may be thought of as his last poem, or his last sermon.

Many of Donne's longer works are shapeless; but his lyrics and sonnets, whether sacred or profane, have one master-quality: strength and economy of design. The mixture of 'false' wit with the true, the rapid zigzags of the thought, and the general strangeness of the style, easily make us overlook this virtue, which was Donne's most valuable lesson to the poets. Study, from this point of view, his much-derided *Valediction: of my Name, in the Window*, or the elaborate *Will*, or the brief *Hymn to God the Father*, tracking the argument, and heeding overture and close; and the rule, everywhere, of the artistic intellect, the mastery of *line*, is evident.

Selections from
JOHN DONNE

SONGS AND SONNETS

Song

GOE, and catche a falling starre,
   Get with child a mandrake roote,
Tell me, where all past yeares are,
   Or who cleft the Divels foot,
Teach me to heare Mermaides singing,   5
   Or to keep off envies stinging,
          And finde
          What winde
Serves to advance an honest minde.

If thou beest borne to strange sights,   10
   Things invisible to see,
Ride ten thousand daies and nights,
   Till age snow white haires on thee,
Thou, when thou retorn'st, wilt tell mee
All strange wonders that befell thee,   15
          And sweare
          No where
Lives a woman true, and faire.

If thou findst one, let mee know,
   Such a Pilgrimage were sweet;   20
Yet doe not, I would not goe,
   Though at next doore wee might meet,
Though shee were true, when you met her,
And last, till you write your letter,
          Yet shee   25
          Will bee
False, ere I come, to two, or three.

Song

SWEETEST love, I do not goe,
    For wearinesse of thee,
Nor in hope the world can show
    A fitter Love for mee;
      But since that I   5
Must dye at last, 'tis best,
To use my selfe in jest
    Thus by fain'd deaths to dye;

Yesternight the Sunne went hence,
    And yet is here to day,   10
He hath no desire nor sense,
    Nor halfe so short a way:
      Then feare not mee,
But beleeve that I shall make
Speedier journeyes, since I take   15
    More wings and spurres then hee.

O how feeble is mans power,
    That if good fortune fall,
Cannot adde another houre,
    Nor a lost houre recall!   20
      But come bad chance,
And wee joyne to'it our strength,
And wee teach it art and length,
    It selfe o'r us to'advance.

When thou sigh'st, thou sigh'st not winde,   25
    But sigh'st my soule away,
When thou weep'st, unkindly kinde,
    My lifes blood doth decay.

It cannot bee
That thou lov'st mee, as thou say'st,   30
If in thine my life thou waste,
   Thou art the best of mee.

Let not thy divining heart
   Forethinke me any ill,
Destiny may take thy part,   35
   And may thy feares fulfill;
     But thinke that wee
Are but turn'd aside to sleepe;
They who one another keepe
   Alive, ne'r parted bee.   40

The Message

SEND home my long strayd eyes to mee,
Which (Oh) too long have dwelt on thee;
Yet since there they have learn'd such ill,
   Such forc'd fashions,
   And false passions,   5
     That they be
     Made by thee
Fit for no good sight, keep them still.

Send home my harmlesse heart againe,
Which no unworthy thought could staine;   10
But if it be taught by thine
   To make jestings
   Of protestings,
     And crosse both
     Word and oath,   15
Keepe it, for then 'tis none of mine.

Yet send me back my heart and eyes,
That I may know, and see thy lyes,
And may laugh and joy, when thou
  Art in anguish   20
  And dost languish
   For some one
   That will none,
Or prove as false as thou art now.

The good-morrow

I WONDER by my troth, what thou, and I
Did, till we lov'd? were we not wean'd till then?
But suck'd on countrey pleasures, childishly?
Or snorted we in the seaven sleepers den?
T'was so; But this, all pleasures fancies bee. 5
If ever any beauty I did see,
Which I desir'd, and got, t'was but a dreame of thee.

And now good morrow to our waking soules,
Which watch not one another out of feare;
For love, all love of other sights controules, 10
And makes one little roome, an every where.
Let sea-discoverers to new worlds have gone,
Let Maps to other, worlds on worlds have showne,
Let us possesse one world, each hath one, and is one.

My face in thine eye, thine in mine appeares, 15
And true plain hearts doe in the faces rest,
Where can we finde two better hemispheares
Without sharpe North, without declining West?
What ever dyes, was not mixt equally;
If our two loves be one, or, thou and I 20
Love so alike, that none doe slacken, none can die.

Break of Daye

(a)

STAY, O sweet, and do not rise,
The light that shines comes from thine eyes;
The day breaks not, it is my heart,
Because that you and I must part.
   Stay, or else my joys will die,   5
   And perish in their infancie.

(b)

'TIS true, 'tis day; what though it be?
O wilt thou therefore rise from me?
Why should we rise, because 'tis light?
Did we lie downe, because 'twas night?
Love which in spight of darknesse brought us hether, 5
Should in despight of light keepe us together.

Light hath no tongue, but is all eye;
If it could speake as well as spie,
This were the worst, that it could say,
That being well, I faine would stay,   10
And that I lov'd my heart and honor so,
That I would not from him, that had them, goe.

Must businesse thee from hence remove?
Oh, that's the worst disease of love,
The poore, the foule, the false, love can   15
Admit, but not the busied man.
He which hath businesse, and makes love, doth doe
Such wrong, as when a maryed man doth wooe.

The Extasie

WHERE, like a pillow on a bed,
    A Pregnant banke swel'd up, to rest
The violets reclining head,
    Sat we two, one anothers best.
Our hands were firmely cimented   5
    With a fast balme, which thence did spring,
Our eye-beames twisted, and did thred
    Our eyes, upon one double string;
So to'entergraft our hands, as yet
    Was all the meanes to make us one,   10
And pictures in our eyes to get
    Was all our propagation.
As 'twixt two equal Armies, Fate
    Suspends uncertaine victorie,
Our soules, (which to advance their state,   15
    Were gone out,) hung 'twixt her, and mee.
And whil'st our soules negotiate there,
    Wee like sepulchrall statues lay;
All day, the same our postures were,
    And wee said nothing, all the day.   20
If any, so by love refin'd,
    That he soules language understood,
And by good love were growen all minde,
    Within convenient distance stood,
He (though he knew not which soule spake,   25
    Because both meant, both spake the same)
Might thence a new concoction take,
    And part farre purer then he came.
This Extasie doth unperplex
    (We said) and tell us what we love,   30

Wee see by this, it was not sexe,
   Wee see, we saw not what did move:
But as all severall soules containe
   Mixture of things, they know not what,
Love, these mixt soules doth mixe againe,   35
   And makes both one, each this and that.
A single violet transplant,
   The strength, the colour, and the size,
(All which before was poore, and scant,)
   Redoubles still, and multiplies.   40
When love, with one another so
   Interinanimates two soules,
That abler soule, which thence doth flow,
   Defects of lonelinesse controules.
Wee then, who are this new soule, know,   45
   Of what we are compos'd, and made,
For, th'Atomies of which we grow,
   Are soules, whom no change can invade.
But O alas, so long, so farre
   Our bodies why doe wee forbeare?   50
They'are ours, though they'are not wee, Wee are
   The intelligences, they the spheare.
We owe them thankes, because they thus,
   Did us, to us, at first convay,
Yeelded their forces, sense, to us,   55
   Nor are drosse to us, but allay.
On man heavens influence workes not so,
   But that it first imprints the ayre,
Soe soule into the soule may flow,
   Though it to body first repaire.   60
As our blood labours to beget
   Spirits, as like soules as it can,
Because such fingers need to knit
   That subtile knot, which makes us man:

So must pure lovers soules descend   65
   T'affections, and to faculties,
Which sense may reach and apprehend,
   Else a great Prince in prison lies.
To'our bodies turne wee then, that so
   Weake men on love reveal'd may looke;   70
Loves mysteries in soules doe grow,
   But yet the body is his booke.
And if some lover, such as wee,
   Have heard this dialogue of one,
Let him still marke us, he shall see   75
   Small change, when we'are to bodies gone.

A Feaver

Oh doe not die, for I shall hate
   All women so, when thou art gone,
That thee I shall not celebrate,
   When I remember, thou wast one.

But yet thou canst not die, I know;   5
   To leave this world behinde, is death,
But when thou from this world wilt goe,
   The whole world vapors with thy breath.

Or if, when thou, the worlds soule, goest,
   It stay, tis but thy carkasse then,   10
The fairest woman, but thy ghost,
   But corrupt wormes, the worthyest men.

O wrangling schooles, that search what fire
   Shall burne this world, had none the wit
Unto this knowledge to aspire,   15
   That this her feaver might be it?

And yet she cannot wast by this,
   Nor long beare this torturing wrong,
For much corruption needfull is
   To fuell such a feaver long.   20

These burning fits but meteors bee,
   Whose matter in thee is soone spent.
Thy beauty,'and all parts, which are thee,
   Are unchangeable firmament.

Yet t'was of my minde, seising thee,   25
   Though it in thee cannot persever.
For I had rather owner bee
   Of thee one houre, then all else ever.

A Valediction: forbidding mourning

As virtuous men passe mildly away,
   And whisper to their soules, to goe,
Whilst some of their sad friends doe say,
   The breath goes now, and some say, no:

So let us melt, and make no noise,   5
   No teare-floods, nor sigh-tempests move,
T'were prophanation of our joyes
   To tell the layetie our love.

Moving of th'earth brings harmes and feares,
   Men reckon what it did and meant,   10
But trepidation of the spheares,
   Though greater farre, is innocent.

Dull sublunary lovers love
   (Whose soule is sense) cannot admit
Absence, because it doth remove   15
   Those things which elemented it.

But we by a love, so much refin'd,
    That our selves know not what it is,
Inter-assured of the mind,
    Care lesse, eyes, lips, and hands to misse.   20

Our two soules therefore, which are one,
    Though I must goe, endure not yet
A breach, but an expansion,
    Like gold to ayery thinnesse beate.

If they be two, they are two so   25
    As stiffe twin compasses are two,
Thy soule the fixt foot, make no show
    To move, but doth, if the'other doe.

And though it in the center sit,
    Yet when the other far doth rome,   30
It leanes, and hearkens after it,
    And growes erect, as that comes home.

Such wilt thou be to mee, who must
    Like th'other foot, obliquely runne;
Thy firmnes makes my circle just,   35
    And makes me end, where I begunne.

The Baite

COME live with mee, and bee my love,
And we will some new pleasures prove
Of golden sands, and christall brookes,
With silken lines, and silver hookes.

There will the river whispering runne   5
Warm'd by thy eyes, more then the Sunne.
And there the'inamor'd fish will stay,
Begging themselves they may betray.

When thou wilt swimme in that live bath,
Each fish, which every channell hath,   10
Will amorously to thee swimme,
Gladder to catch thee, then thou him.

If thou, to be so seene, beest loath,
By Sunne, or Moone, thou darknest both,
And if my selfe have leave to see,   15
I need not their light, having thee.

Let others freeze with angling reeds,
And cut their legges, with shells and weeds
Or treacherously poore fish beset,
With strangling snare, or windowie net: 20

Let coarse bold hands, from slimy nest
The bedded fish in banks out-wrest,
Or curious traitors, sleavesilke flies
Bewitch poore fishes wandring eyes.

For thee, thou needst no such deceit,   25
For thou thy selfe art thine owne bait;
That fish, that is not catch'd thereby,
Alas, is wiser farre then I.

Womans constancy

Now thou hast lov'd me one whole day,
To morrow when thou leav'st, what wilt thou say?
Wilt thou then Antedate some new made vow?
        Or say that now
We are not just those persons, which we were?   5
Or, that oathes made in reverentiall feare
Of Love, and his wrath, any may forsweare?
Or, as true deaths, true maryages untie,

So lovers contracts, images of those,
Binde but till sleep, deaths image, them unloose?   10
        Or, your owne end to Justifie,
For having purpos'd change, and falsehood; you
Can have no way but falsehood to be true?
Vaine lunatique, against these scapes I could
        Dispute, and conquer, if I would,   15
        Which I abstaine to doe,
For by to morrow, I may thinke so too.

The Sunne Rising

    BUSIE old foole, unruly Sunne,
      Why dost thou thus,
Through windowes, and through curtaines call on us?
Must to thy motions lovers seasons run?
      Sawcy pedantique wretch, goe chide   5
      Late schoole boyes, and sowre prentices,
  Goe tell Court-huntsmen, that the King will ride,
  Call countrey ants to harvest offices;
Love, all alike, no season knowes, nor clyme,
Nor houres, dayes, moneths, which are the rags of time.

    Thy beames, so reverend, and strong   11
      Why shouldst thou thinke?
I could eclipse and cloud them with a winke,
But that I would not lose her sight so long:
      If her eyes have not blinded thine,   15
      Looke, and to morrow late, tell mee,
  Whether both the'India's of spice and Myne
  Be where thou leftst them, or lie here with mee.
Aske for those Kings whom thou saw'st yesterday,
And thou shalt heare, All here in one bed lay.   20

She'is all States, and all Princes, I,
　　Nothing else is.
Princes doe but play us; compar'd to this,
All honor's mimique; All wealth alchimie.
　　Thou sunne art halfe as happy'as wee,　　　25
　　In that the world's contracted thus.
　Thine age askes ease, and since thy duties bee
　To warme the world, that's done in warming us.
Shine here to us, and thou art every where;
This bed thy center is, these walls, thy spheare.　　30

The Indifferent

I CAN love both faire and browne,
Her whom abundance melts, and her whom want betraies,
Her who loves lonenesse best, and her who maskes and
　　plaies,
Her whom the country form'd, and whom the town,
Her who beleeves, and her who tries,　　　5
Her who still weepes with spungie eyes,
And her who is dry corke, and never cries;
I can love her, and her, and you and you,
I can love any, so she be not true.

Will no other vice content you?　　　10
Wil it not serve your turn to do, as did your mothers?
Or have you all old vices spent, and now would finde out
　　others?
Or doth a feare, that men are true, torment you?
Oh we are not, be not you so,
Let mee, and doe you, twenty know.　　　15
Rob mee, but binde me not, and let me goe.
Must I, who came to travaile thorow you,
Grow your fixt subject, because you are true?

Venus heard me sigh this song,
And by Loves sweetest Part, Variety, she swore,   20
She heard not this till now; and that it should be so no
    more.
She went, examin'd, and return'd ere long,
And said, alas, Some two or three
Poore Heretiques in love there bee,
Which thinke to stablish dangerous constancie.   25
But I have told them, since you will be true,
You shall be true to them, who'are false to you.

The Canonization

FOR Godsake hold your tongue, and let me love,
    Or chide my palsie, or my gout,
My five gray haires, or ruin'd fortune flout,
    With wealth your state, your minde with Arts improve,
        Take you a course, get you a place,   5
        Observe his honour, or his grace,
Or the Kings reall, or his stamped face
    Contemplate, what you will, approve,
    So you will let me love.

Alas, alas, who's injur'd by my love?   10
    What merchants ships have my sighs drown'd?
Who saies my teares have overflow'd his ground?
    When did my colds a forward spring remove?
        When did the heats which my veines fill
        Adde one more to the plaguie Bill?   15
Soldiers finde warres, and Lawyers finde out still
    Litigious men, which quarrels move,
    Though she and I do love.

Call us what you will, wee are made such by love;
  Call her one, mee another flye,   20
We'are Tapers too, and at our owne cost die,
    And wee in us finde the'Eagle and the Dove.
      The Phœnix ridle hath more wit
      By us, we two being one, are it.
So, to one neutrall thing both sexes fit.   25
  Wee dye and rise the same, and prove
  Mysterious by this love.

Wee can dye by it, if not live by love,
  And if unfit for tombes and hearse
Our legend bee, it will be fit for verse;   30
    And if no peece of Chronicle wee prove,
      We'll build in sonnets pretty roomes;
      As well a well wrought urne becomes
The greatest ashes, as halfe-acre tombes,
    And by these hymnes, all shall approve   35
    Us *Canoniz'd* for Love:

And thus invoke us; You whom reverend love
  Made one anothers hermitage;
You, to whom love was peace, that now is rage;
    Who did the whole worlds soule contract, and drove 40
      Into the glasses of your eyes
      So made such mirrors, and such spies,
That they did all to you epitomize,
    Countries, Townes, Courts: Beg from above
    A patterne of your love!   45

The triple Foole

    I ᴀᴍ two fooles, I know,
    For loving, and for saying so
      In whining Poëtry;

But where's that wiseman, that would not be I,
    If she would not deny ?   5
Then as th'earths inward narrow crooked lanes
Do purge sea waters fretfull salt away,
    I thought, if I could draw my paines,
Through Rimes vexation, I should them allay,
Griefe brought to numbers cannot be so fierce,   10
For, he tames it, that fetters it in verse.

    But when I have done so,
Some man, his art and voice to show,
    Doth Set and sing my paine,
And, by delighting many, frees againe   15
    Griefe, which verse did restraine.
To Love, and Griefe tribute of Verse belongs,
But not of such as pleases when'tis read,
    Both are increased by such songs:
For both their triumphs so are published,   20
And I, which was two fooles, do so grow three;
Who are a little wise, the best fooles bee.

The Anniversarie

ALL Kings, and all their favorites,
    All glory of honors, beauties, wits,
The Sun it selfe, which makes times, as they passe,
Is elder by a yeare, now, then it was
When thou and I first one another saw: 5
All other things, to their destruction draw,
    Only our love hath no decay ;
This, no to morrow hath, nor yesterday,
Running it never runs from us away,
But truly keepes his first, last, everlasting day.   10

Two graves must hide thine and my coarse,
  If one might, death were no divorce:
Alas, as well as other Princes, wee,
(Who Prince enough in one another bee,)
Must leave at last in death, these eyes, and eares,   15
Oft fed with true oathes, and with sweet salt teares;
  But soules where nothing dwells but love
(All other thoughts being inmates) then shall prove
This, or a love increased there above,
When bodies to their graves, soules from their graves
    remove.   20

And then wee shall be throughly blest,
  But wee no more, then all the rest;
Here upon earth, we'are Kings, and none but wee
Can be such Kings, nor of such subjects bee;
Who is so safe as wee? where none can doe   25
Treason to us, except one of us two.
  True and false feares let us refraine,
Let us love nobly, and live, and adde againe
Yeares and yeares unto yeares, till we attaine
To write threescore: this is the second of our raigne.   30

Twicknam garden

BLASTED with sighs, and surrounded with teares,
    Hither I come to seeke the spring,
    And at mine eyes, and at mine eares,
Receive such balmes, as else cure every thing;
    But O, selfe traytor, I do bring   5
The spider love, which transubstantiates all,
    And can convert Manna to gall,
And that this place may thoroughly be thought
    True Paradise. I have the serpent brought.

'Twere wholsomer for mee, that winter did   10
   Benight the glory of this place,
   And that a grave frost did forbid
These trees to laugh, and mocke mee to my face;
   But that I may not this disgrace
Indure, nor yet leave loving, Love let mee   15
   Some senslesse peece of this place bee;
Make me a mandrake, so I may grow here,
   Or a stone fountaine weeping out my yeare.

Hither with christall vyals, lovers come,
   And take my teares, which are loves wine,   20
   And try your mistresse Teares at home,
For all are false, that tast not just like mine;
   Alas, hearts do not in eyes shine,
Nor can you more judge womans thoughts by teares,
   Then by her shadow, what she weares.   25
O perverse sexe, where none is true but shee,
   Who's therefore true, because her truth kills mee.

From *A Valediction: of the booke*

I'LL tell thee now (deare Love) what thou shalt doe
   To anger destiny, as she doth us,
   How I shall stay, though she Esloygne me thus,
And how posterity shall know it too;
      How thine may out-endure   5
      Sybills glory, and obscure
      Her who from Pindar could allure,
   And her, through whose helpe *Lucan* is not lame,
And her, whose booke (they say) *Homer* did finde, and name.

Study our manuscripts, those Myriades   10
   Of letters, which have past twixt thee and mee,
   Thence write our Annals, and in them will bee
To all whom loves subliming fire invades,

Rule and example found;
There, the faith of any ground 15
No schismatique will dare to wound,
That sees, how Love this grace to us affords,
To make, to keep, to use, to be these his Records.

This Booke, as long-liv'd as the elements,
Or as the worlds forme, this all-graved tome 20
In cypher writ, or new made Idiome,
(Wee for loves clergie only'are instruments:)
When this booke is made thus,
Should againe the ravenous
Vandals and Goths inundate us, 25
Learning were safe; in this our Universe
Schooles might learne Sciences, Spheares Musick, Angels
Verse.

Here Loves Divines, (since all Divinity
Is love or wonder) may finde all they seeke,
Whether abstract spirituall love they like, 30
Their Soules exhal'd with what they do not see,
Or, loth so to amuze
Faiths infirmitie, they chuse
Something which they may see and use;
For, though minde be the heaven, where love doth sit, 35
Beauty a convenient type may be to figure it.

The Dreame

DEARE love, for nothing lesse then thee
Would I have broke this happy dreame,
It was a theame
For reason, much too strong for phantasie,

Therefore thou wakd'st me wisely; yet   5
My Dreame thou brok'st not, but continued'st it,
Thou art so truth, that thoughts of thee suffice,
To make dreames truths; and fables histories;
Enter these armes, for since thou thoughtst it best,
Not to dreame all my dreame, let's act the rest.   10

As lightning, or a Tapers light,
Thine eyes, and not thy noise wak'd mee;
      Yet I thought thee
(For thou lovest truth) an Angell, at first sight,
But when I saw thou sawest my heart,   15
And knew'st my thoughts, beyond an Angels art,
When thou knew'st what I dreamt, when thou knew'st when
Excesse of joy would wake me, and cam'st then,
I must confesse, it could not chuse but bee
Prophane, to thinke thee any thing but thee.   20

Comming and staying show'd thee, thee,
But rising makes me doubt, that now,
      Thou art not thou.
That love is weake, where feare's as strong as hee;
'Tis not all spirit, pure, and brave,   25
If mixture it of *Feare, Shame, Honor*, have.
Perchance as torches which must ready bee,
Men light and put out, so thou deal'st with mee,
Thou cam'st to kindle, goest to come; Then I
Will dreame that hope againe, but else would die.   30

A nocturnall upon S. Lucies *day,* *Being the shortest day*

Tis the yeares midnight, and it is the dayes,
   Lucies, who scarce seaven houres herself unmaskes,
     The Sunne is spent, and now his flasks
     Send forth light squibs, no constant rayes;

The worlds whole sap is sunke: 5
The generall balme th'hydroptique earth hath drunk,
Whither, as to the beds-feet, life is shrunke,
Dead and enterr'd; yet all these seeme to laugh,
Compar'd with mee, who am their Epitaph.

Study me then, you who shall lovers bee   10
At the next world, that is, at the next Spring:
   For I am every dead thing,
   In whom love wrought new Alchimie.
     For his art did expresse
A quintessence even from nothingnesse,   15
From dull privations, and leane emptinesse
He ruin'd mee, and I am re-begot
Of absence, darknesse, death; things which are not.

All others, from all things, draw all that's good,
Life, soule, forme, spirit, whence they beeing have;   20
   I, by loves limbecke, am the grave
   Of all, that's nothing. Oft a flood
     Have wee two wept, and so
Drownd the whole world, us two; oft did we grow
To be two Chaosses, when we did show   25
Care to ought else; and often absences
Withdrew our soules, and made us carcasses.

But I am by her death, (which word wrongs her)
Of the first nothing, the Elixer grown;
   Were I a man, that I were one,   30
   I needs must know; I should preferre,
     If I were any beast,
Some ends, some means; Yea plants, yea stones detest,
And love; All, all some properties invest;
If I an ordinary nothing were,
As shadow, a light, and body must be here.

But I am None; nor will my Sunne renew.
You lovers, for whose sake, the lesser Sunne
  At this time to the Goat is runne
   To fetch new lust, and give it you,   40
     Enjoy your summer, all;
Since shee enjoyes her long nights festivall,
Let mee prepare towards her, and let mee call
This houre her Vigill, and her Eve, since this
Both the yeares, and the dayes deep midnight is.   45

The Apparition

WHEN by thy scorne, O murdresse I am dead,
And that thou thinkst thee free
From all solicitation from mee,
Then shall my ghost come to thy bed,
And thee, fain'd vestall, in worse armes shall see;   5
Then thy sicke taper will begin to winke,
And he, whose thou art then, being tyr'd before,
Will, if thou stirre, or pinch to wake him, thinke
    Thou call'st for more,
And in false sleepe will from thee shrinke,   10
And then poore Aspen wretch, neglected thou
Bath'd in a cold quicksilver sweat wilt lye
    A veryer ghost then I;
What I will say, I will not tell thee now,
Lest that preserve thee'; and since my love is spent, 15
I'had rather thou shouldst painfully repent,
Then by my threatnings rest still innocent.

Loves Deitie

I LONG to talke with some old lovers ghost,
　Who dyed before the god of Love was borne:
I cannot thinke that hee, who then lov'd most,
　Sunke so low, as to love one which did scorne.
But since this god produc'd a destinie,　　　　　　5
And that vice-nature, custome, lets it be;
　I must love her, that loves not mee.

Sure, they which made him god, meant not so much,
　Nor he, in his young godhead practis'd it;
But when an even flame two hearts did touch,　　10
　His office was indulgently to fit
Actives to passives. Correspondencie
Only his subject was; It cannot bee
　Love, till I love her, that loves mee.

But every moderne god will now extend　　　　　15
　His vast prerogative, as far as Jove.
To rage, to lust, to write to, to commend,
　All is the purlewe of the God of Love.
Oh were wee wak'ned by this Tyrannie
To ungod this child againe, it could not bee　　20
　I should love her, who loves not mee.

Rebell and Atheist too, why murmure I,
　As though I felt the worst that love could doe?
Love might make me leave loving, or might trie
　A deeper plague, to make her love me too,　　25
Which, since she loves before, I'am loth to see;
Falshood is worse then hate; and that must bee,
　If shee whom I love, should love mee.

The Will

BEFORE I sigh my last gaspe, let me breath,
Great love, some Legacies; Here I bequeath
Mine eyes to *Argus*, if mine eyes can see,
If they be blinde, then Love, I give them thee;
My tongue to Fame; to'Embassadours mine eares;   5
   To women or the sea, my teares.
Thou, Love, hast taught mee heretofore
By making mee serve her who'had twenty more,
That I should give to none, but such, as had too much
    before.

My constancie I to the planets give;   10
My truth to them, who at the Court doe live;
Mine ingenuity and opennesse,
To Jesuites; to Buffones my pensivenesse;
My silence to'any, who abroad hath beene;
   My mony to a Capuchin.   15
Thou Love taught'st me, by appointing mee
To love there, where no love receiv'd can be,
Onely to give to such as have an incapacitie.

My faith I give to Roman Catholiques;
All my good works unto the Schismaticks   20
Of Amsterdam; my best civility
And Courtship, to an Universitie;
My modesty I give to souldiers bare;
   My patience let gamesters share.
Thou Love taughtst mee, by making mee   25
 Love her that holds my love disparity,
Onely to give to those that count my gifts indignity

I give my reputation to those
Which were my friends; Mine industrie to foes;
To Schoolemen I bequeath my doubtfulnesse;   30
My sicknesse to Physitians, or excesse;
To Nature, all that I in Ryme have writ;
    And to my company my wit.
Thou Love, by making mee adore
Her, who begot this love in mee before,   35
Taughtst me to make, as though I gave, when I did but
    restore.

To him for whom the passing bell next tolls,
I give my physick bookes; my writen rowles
Of Morall counsels, I to Bedlam give;
My brazen medals, unto them which live   40
In want of bread; To them which passe among
    All forrainers, mine English tongue.
Thou, Love, by making mee love one
Who thinkes her friendship a fit portion
For yonger lovers, dost my gifts thus disproportion.   45

Therefore I'll give no more; But I'll undoe
The world by dying; because love dies too.
Then all your beauties will bee no more worth
Then gold in Mines, where none doth draw it forth:
And all your graces no more use shall have   50
    Then a Sun dyall in a grave.
Thou Love taughtst mee, by making mee
Love her, who doth neglect both mee and thee,
To 'invent, and practise this one way, to 'annihilate all three.

The Funerall

WHO ever comes to shroud me, do not harme
    Nor question much
That subtile wreath of haire, which crowns my arme;
The mystery, the signe you must not touch,
    For 'tis my outward Soule,   5
Viceroy to that, which then to heaven being gone,
    Will leave this to controule,
And keepe these limbes, her Provinces, from dissolution.

For if the sinewie thread my braine lets fall
    Through every part,   10
Can tye those parts, and make mee one of all;
These haires which upward grew, and strength and art
    Have from a better braine,
Can better do'it; Except she meant that I
    By this should know my pain,   15
As prisoners then are manacled, when they'are condemn'd
    to die.

What ere shee meant by'it, bury it with me,
    For since I am
Loves martyr, it might breed idolatrie,
If into others hands these Reliques came;   20
    As 'twas humility
To afford to it all that a Soule can doe,
    So, 'tis some bravery,
That since you would save none of mee, I bury some of you.

The Relique

WHEN my grave is broke up againe
Some second ghest to entertaine,
(For graves have learn'd that woman-head
To be to more then one a Bed)
    And he that digs it, spies   5
A bracelet of bright haire about the bone,
    Will he not let'us alone,
And thinke that there a loving couple lies,
Who thought that this device might be some way
To make their soules, at the last busie day,   10
Meet at this grave, and make a little stay?

    If this fall in a time, or land,
    Where mis-devotion doth command,
    Then, he that digges us up, will bring
    Us, to the Bishop, and the King,   15
    To make us Reliques; then
Thou shalt be a Mary Magdalen, and I
    A something else thereby;
All women shall adore us, and some men;
And since at such time, miracles are sought,   20
I would have that age by this paper taught
What miracles wee harmelesse lovers wrought.

    First, we lov'd well and faithfully,
    Yet knew not what wee lov'd, nor why,
    Difference of sex no more wee knew,   25
    Then our Guardian Angells doe;
    Comming and going, wee
Perchance might kisse, but not between those meales;
    Our hands ne'r toucht the seales,

Which nature, injur'd by late law, sets free: 30
These miracles wee did; but now alas,
All measure, and all language, I should passe,
Should I tell what a miracle shee was.

The Blossome

LITTLE think'st thou, poore flower,
  Whom I have watch'd sixe or seaven dayes,
And seene thy birth, and seene what every houre
Gave to thy growth, thee to this height to raise,
And now dost laugh and triumph on this bough, 5
      Little think'st thou
That it will freeze anon, and that I shall
To morrow finde thee falne, or not at all.

Little think'st thou poore heart
  That labour'st yet to nestle thee, 10
And think'st by hovering here to get a part
In a forbidden or forbidding tree,
And hop'st her stiffenesse by long siege to bow:
      Little think'st thou,
That thou to morrow, ere that Sunne doth wake, 15
Must with this Sunne, and mee a journey take.

But thou which lov'st to bee
  Subtile to plague thy selfe, wilt say,
Alas, if you must goe, what's that to mee?
Here lyes my businesse, and here I will stay: 20
You goe to friends, whose love and meanes present
      Various content
To your eyes, eares, and tongue, and every part.
If then your body goe, what need you a heart?

Well then, stay here; but know,   25
  When thou hast stayd and done thy most;
A naked thinking heart, that makes no show,
Is to a woman, but a kinde of Ghost;
How shall shee know my heart; or having none,
      Know thee for one?   30
Practise may make her know some other part,
But take my word, shee doth not know a Heart.

  Meet mee at London, then,
  Twenty dayes hence, and thou shalt see
Mee fresher, and more fat, by being with men,   35
Then if I had staid still with her and thee.
For Gods sake, if you can, be you so too:
    I would give you
There, to another friend, whom wee shall finde
As glad to have my body, as my minde.   40

The Prohibition

TAKE heed of loving mee,
  At least remember, I forbade it thee;
Not that I shall repaire my'unthrifty wast
Of Breath and Blood, upon thy sighes, and teares,
By being to thee then what to me thou wast;   5
But, so great Joy, our life at once outweares,
Then, least thy love, by my death, frustrate bee,
If thou love mee, take heed of loving mee.

  Take heed of hating mee,
Or too much triumph in the Victorie.   10
Not that I shall be mine owne officer,
And hate with hate againe retaliate;

But thou wilt lose the stile of conquerour,
If I, thy conquest, perish by thy hate.
Then, least my being nothing lessen thee,   15
If thou hate mee, take heed of hating mee.

       Yet, love and hate mee too,
So, these extreames shall ne'r their office doe;
Love mee, that I may die the gentler way;
Hate mee, because thy love'is too great for mee;   20
Or let these two, themselves, not me decay;
So shall I, live, thy Stage, not triumph bee;
Lest thou thy love and hate and mee undoe,
To let mee live, O love and hate mee too.

The Expiration

So, so, breake off this last lamenting kisse,
   Which sucks two soules, and vapors Both away,
Turne thou ghost that way, and let mee turne this,
   And let our selves benight our happiest day,
We ask'd none leave to love; nor will we owe   5
   Any, so cheape a death, as saying, Goe;

Goe; and if that word have not quite kil'd thee,
   Ease mee with death, by bidding mee goe too.
Or, if it have, let my word worke on mee,
   And a just office on a murderer doe.   10
Except it be too late, to kill me so,
   Being double dead, going, and bidding, goe.

A Lecture upon the Shadow

STAND still, and I will read to thee
A Lecture, Love, in loves philosophy.
    These three houres that we have spent,
    Walking here, Two shadowes went
Along with us, which we our selves produc'd;   5
But, now the Sunne is just above our head,
    We doe those shadowes tread;
    And to brave clearnesse all things are reduc'd.
  So whilst our infant loves did grow,
  Disguises did, and shadowes, flow,   10
  From us, and our cares; but, now 'tis not so.

That love hath not attain'd the high'st degree,
Which is still diligent lest others see.

Except our loves at this noone stay,
We shall new shadowes make the other way.   15
    As the first were made to blinde
    Others; these which come behinde
Will worke upon our selves, and blind our eyes.
If our loves faint, and westwardly decline;
    To me thou, falsly, thine,   20
    And I to thee mine actions shall disguise.
  The morning shadowes weare away,
  But these grow longer all the day,
  But oh, loves day is short, if love decay.

Love is a growing, or full constant light;   25
And his first minute, after noone, is night.

ELEGIES

ELEGIE V

His Picture

HERE take my Picture; though I bid farewell,
Thine, in my heart, where my soule dwels, shall dwell.
'Tis like me now, but I dead, 'twill be more
When wee are shadowes both, then 'twas before.
When weather-beaten I come backe; my hand,   5
Perhaps with rude oares torne, or Sun beams tann'd,
My face and brest of hairecloth, and my head
With cares rash sodaine stormes, being o'rspread,
My body'a sack of bones, broken within,
And powders blew staines scatter'd on my skinne;   10
If rivall fooles taxe thee to'have lov'd a man,
So foule, and course, as, Oh, I may seeme than,
This shall say what I was: and thou shalt say,
Doe his hurts reach mee? doth my worth decay?
Or doe they reach his judging minde, that hee   15
Should now love lesse, what hee did love to see?
That which in him was faire and delicate,
Was but the milke, which in loves childish state
Did nurse it: who now is growne strong enough
To feed on that, which to disus'd tasts seemes tough.   20

ELEGIE XII

His parting from her

SINCE she must go, and I must mourn, come Night,
Environ me with darkness, whilst I write:
Shadow that hell unto me, which alone
I am to suffer when my Love is gone.

Alas the darkest Magick cannot do it,   5
Thou and greate Hell to boot are shadows to it.
Should *Cinthia* quit thee, *Venus*, and each starre,
It would not forme one thought dark as mine are.
I could lend thee obscureness now, and say,
Out of my self, There should be no more Day,   10
Such is already my felt want of sight,
Did not the fires within me force a light.
Oh Love, that fire and darkness should be mixt,
Or to thy Triumphs soe strange torments fixt!
Is't because thou thy self art blind, that wee   15
Thy Martyrs must no more each other see?
Or tak'st thou pride to break us on the wheel,
And view old Chaos in the Pains we feel?
Or have we left undone some mutual Right,
Through holy fear, that merits thy despight?   20
No, no. The falt was mine, impute it to me,
Or rather to conspiring destinie,
Which (since I lov'd for forme before) decreed,
That I should suffer when I lov'd indeed:
And therefore now, sooner then I can say,   25
I saw the golden fruit, 'tis rapt away.
Or as I had watcht one drop in a vast stream,
And I left wealthy only in a dream.
Yet Love, thou'rt blinder then thy self in this,
To vex my Dove-like friend for my amiss: 30
And, where my own sad truth may expiate
Thy wrath, to make her fortune run my fate:
So blinded Justice doth, when Favorites fall,
Strike them, their house, their friends, their followers all.
Was't not enough that thou didst dart thy fires   35
Into our blouds, inflaming our desires,
And made'st us sigh and glow, and pant, and burn,
And then thy self into our flame did'st turn?

Was't not enough, that thou didst hazard us
To paths in love so dark, so dangerous: 40
And those so ambush'd round with houshold spies,
And over all, the husbands towred eyes
Inflam'd with th'oughlie sweat of jealousie:
Yet went we not still on with Constancie?
Have we not kept our guards, like spie on spie?   45
Had correspondence whilst the foe stood by?
Stoln (more to sweeten them) our many blisses
Of meetings, conference, embracements, kisses?
Shadow'd with negligence our most respects?
Varied our language through all dialects,   50
Of becks, winks, looks, and often under-boards
Spoak dialogues with our feet far from our words?
Have we prov'd all these secrets of our Art,
Yea, thy pale inwards, and thy panting heart?
And, after all this passed Purgatory,   55
Must sad divorce make us the vulgar story?
First let our eyes be rivited quite through
Our turning brains, and both our lips grow to:
Let our armes clasp like Ivy, and our fear
Freese us together, that we may stick here,   60
Till Fortune, that would rive us, with the deed
Strain her eyes open, and it make them bleed:
For Love it cannot be, whom hitherto
I have accus'd, should such a mischief doe.
Oh Fortune, thou'rt not worth my least exclame,   65
And plague enough thou hast in thy own shame.
Do thy great worst, my friend and I have armes,
Though not against thy strokes, against thy harmes.
Rend us in sunder, thou canst not divide
Our bodies so, but that our souls are ty'd,   70
And we can love by letters still and gifts,
And thoughts and dreams; Love never wanteth shifts.

I will not look upon the quickning Sun,
But straight her beauty to my sense shall run;
Thy ayre shall note her soft, the fire most pure;   75
Water suggest her clear, and the earth sure.
Time shall not lose our passages; the Spring
How fresh our love was in the beginning;
The Summer how it ripened in the eare;
And Autumn, what our golden harvests were.   80
The Winter I'll not think on to spite thee,
But count it a lost season, so shall shee.
And dearest Friend, since we must part, drown night
With hope of Day, burthens well born are light.
Though cold and darkness longer hang somewhere,   85
Yet *Phoebus* equally lights all the Sphere.
And what he cannot in like Portions pay,
The world enjoyes in Mass, and so we may.
Be then ever your self, and let no woe
Win on your health, your youth, your beauty: so   90
Declare your self base fortunes Enemy,
No less by your contempt then constancy:
That I may grow enamoured on your mind,
When my own thoughts I there reflected find.
For this to th'comfort of my Dear I vow,   95
My Deeds shall still be what my words are now;
The Poles shall move to teach me ere I start;
And when I change my Love, I'll change my heart;
Nay, if I wax but cold in my desire,
Think, heaven hath motion lost, and the world, fire: 100
Much more I could, but many words have made
That, oft, suspected which men would perswade;
Take therefore all in this: I love so true,
As I will never look for less in you.

EPITHALAMIONS

An Epithalamion, Or mariage Song on the Lady Elizabeth, *and* Count Palatine *being married on St.* Valentines *day*

I

HAILE Bishop Valentine, whose day this is,
    All the Aire is thy Diocis,
    And all the chirping Choristers
And other birds are thy Parishioners,
        Thou marryest every yeare   5
The Lirique Larke, and the grave whispering Dove,
The Sparrow that neglects his life for love,
The household Bird, with the red stomacher,
        Thou mak'st the black bird speed as soone,
As doth the Goldfinch, or the Halcyon;   10
The husband cocke lookes out, and straight is sped,
And meets his wife, which brings her feather-bed.
This day more cheerfully then ever shine,
This day, which might enflame thy self, Old Valentine.

II

Till now, Thou warmd'st with multiplying loves   15
    Two larkes, two sparrowes, or two Doves,
    All that is nothing unto this,
For thou this day couplest two Phœnixes;
        Thou mak'st a Taper see
What the sunne never saw, and what the Arke   20
(Which was of foules, and beasts, the cage, and park,)
Did not containe, one bed containes, through Thee,
        Two Phœnixes, whose joyned breasts
Are unto one another mutuall nests,
Where motion kindles such fires, as shall give   25
Yong Phœnixes, and yet the old shall live.
Whose love and courage never shall decline,
But make the whole year through, thy day, O Valentine.

III

Up then faire Phœnix Bride, frustrate the Sunne,
    Thy selfe from thine affection   30
    Takest warmth enough, and from thine eye
All lesser birds will take their Jollitie.
        Up, up, faire Bride, and call,
Thy starres, from out their severall boxes, take
Thy Rubies, Pearles, and Diamonds forth, and
    make   35
Thy selfe a constellation, of them All,
    And by their blazing, signifie,
That a Great Princess falls, but doth not die;
Bee thou a new starre, that to us portends
Ends of much wonder; And be Thou those ends.   40
Since thou dost this day in new glory shine,
May all men date Records, from this thy Valentine.

IIII

Come forth, come forth, and as one glorious flame
    Meeting Another, growes the same,
    So meet thy Fredericke, and so   45
To an unseparable union growe.
        Since separation
Falls not on such things as are infinite,
Nor things which are but one, can disunite,
You'are twice inseparable, great, and one;   50
    Goe then to where the Bishop staies,
To make you one, his way, which divers waies
Must be effected; and when all is past,
And that you'are one, by hearts and hands made
    fast,
You two have one way left, your selves to'entwine, 55
Besides this Bishops knot, or Bishop Valentine,

V

But oh, what ailes the Sunne, that here he staies,
   Longer to day, then other daies?
   Staies he new light from these to get?
And finding here such store, is loth to set?   60
   And why doe you two walke,
So slowly pac'd in this procession?
Is all your care but to be look'd upon,
And be to others spectacle, and talke?
   The feast, with gluttonous delaies,   65
Is eaten, and too long their meat they praise,
The masquers come too late, and'I thinke, will stay,
Like Fairies, till the Cock crow them away.
Alas, did not Antiquity assigne
A night, as well as day, to thee, O Valentine?   70

VI

They did, and night is come; and yet wee see
   Formalities retarding thee.
   What meane these Ladies, which (as though
They were to take a clock in peeces,) goe
   So nicely about the Bride;   75
A Bride, before a good night could be said,
Should vanish from her cloathes, into her bed,
As Soules from bodies steale, and are not spy'd.
   But now she is laid; What though shee bee?
Yet there are more delayes, For, where is he?
He comes, and passes through Spheare after Spheare,   80
First her sheetes, then her Armes, then any where.
Let not this day, then, but this night be thine,
Thy day was but the eve to this, O Valentine.

VII

Here lyes a shee Sunne, and a hee Moone here,   85
  She gives the best light to his Spheare,
  Or each is both, and all, and so
They unto one another nothing owe,
  And yet they doe, but are
So just and rich in that coyne which they pay,   90
That neither would, nor needs forbeare, nor stay;
Neither desires to be spar'd, nor to spare,
  They quickly pay their debt, and then
Take no acquittances, but pay again;
They pay, they give, they lend, and so let fall   95
No such occasion to be liberall.
More truth, more courage in these two do shine,
Then all thy turtles have, and sparrows, Valentine.

VIII

And by this act of these two Phenixes
  Nature againe restored is,   100
  For since these two are two no more,
Ther's but one Phenix still, as was before.
  Rest now at last, and wee
As Satyres watch the Sunnes uprise, will stay
Waiting, when your eyes opened, let out day,   105
Onely desir'd, because your face wee see;
  Others neare you shall whispering speake,
And wagers lay, at which side day will breake,
And win by'observing, then, whose hand it is
That opens first a curtaine, hers or his;   110
This will be tryed to morrow after nine,
Till which houre, wee thy day enlarge, O Valentine.

Epithalamion made at Lincolnes Inne

THE Sun-beames in the East are spred,
Leave, leave, faire Bride, your solitary bed,
  No more shall you returne to it alone,
It nourseth sadnesse, and your bodies print,
Like to a grave, the yielding downe doth dint;   5
    You and your other you meet there anon;
    Put forth, put forth that warme balme-breathing thigh,
Which when next time you in these sheets wil smother,
    There it must meet another,
        Which never was, but must be, oft, more nigh;   10
Come glad from thence, goe gladder then you came,
To day put on perfection, and a womans name.

Daughters of London, you which bee
Our Golden Mines, and furnish'd Treasurie,
  You which are Angels, yet still bring with you   15
Thousands of Angels on your mariage daies,
Help with your presence, and devise to praise
  These rites, which also unto you grow due;
  Conceitedly dresse her, and be assign'd,
By you, fit place for every flower and jewell,   20
  Make her for love fit fewell
      As gay as Flora, and as rich as Inde;
So may shee faire and rich, in nothing lame,
To day put on perfection, and a womans name.

And you frolique Patricians,   25
Sonnes of those Senators, wealths deep oceans,
  Ye painted courtiers, barrels of others wits,
Yee country men, who but your beasts love none,
Yee of those fellowships whereof hee's one,
  Of study and play made strange Hermaphrodits,   30
  Here shine; This Bridegroom to the Temple bring.

Loe, in yon path which store of straw'd flowers graceth,
   The sober virgin paceth;
      Except my sight faile, 'tis no other thing;
Weep not nor blush, here is no griefe nor shame,   35
To day put on perfection, and a womans name.

Thy two-leav'd gates faire Temple unfold,
And these two in thy sacred bosome hold,
   Till, mystically joyn'd, but one they bee;
Then may thy leane and hunger-starved wombe   40
Long time expect their bodies and their tombe,
   Long after their owne parents fatten thee.
   All elder claimes, and all cold barrennesse,
All yeelding to new loves bee far for ever,
      Which might these two dissever,   45
         Alwaies all th'other may each one possesse;
For, the best Bride, best worthy of praise and fame,
To day puts on perfection, and a womans name.

Winter dayes bring much delight,
Not for themselves, but for they soon bring night;   50
   Other sweets wait thee then these diverse meats,
Other disports then dancing jollities,
Other love tricks then glancing with the eyes,
   But that the Sun still in our halfe Spheare sweates;
      Hee flies in winter, but he now stands still,   55
Yet shadowes turne; Noone point he hath attain'd,
   His steeds will bee restrain'd,
      But gallop lively downe the Westerne hill;
Thou shalt, when he hath runne the worlds half frame,
To night put on perfection, and a womans name.   60

The amorous evening starre is rose,
Why then should not our amorous starre inclose
   Her selfe in her wish'd bed? Release your strings

Musicians, and dancers take some truce
With these your pleasing labours, for great use   65
  As much wearinesse as perfection brings;
    You, and not only you, but all toyl'd beasts
Rest duly; at night all their toyles are dispensed;
But in their beds commenced
    Are other labours, and more dainty feasts;   70
She goes a maid, who, least she turne the same,
To night puts on perfection, and a womans name.

Thy virgins girdle now untie,
And in thy nuptiall bed (loves altar) lye
  A pleasing sacrifice; now dispossesse   75
Thee of these chaines and robes which were put on
T'adorne the day, not thee; for thou, alone,
  Like vertue'and truth, art best in nakednesse;
    This bed is onely to virginitie
A grave, but, to a better state, a cradle;   80
Till now thou wast but able
  To be what now thou art; then that by thee
No more be said, *I may bee*, but, *I am*,
To night put on perfection, and a womans name.

Even like a faithful man content,   85
That this life for a better should be spent;
  So, shee a mothers rich stile doth preferre,
And at the Bridegroomes wish'd approach doth lye,
Like an appointed lambe, when tenderly
  The priest comes on his knees t'embowell her;   90
    Now sleep or watch with more joy; and O light
Of heaven, to morrow rise thou hot, and early;
This Sun will love so dearely
    Her rest, that long, long we shall want her sight;
Wonders are wrought, for shee which had no maime,   95
To night puts on perfection, and a womans name.

SATYRES

Satyre III

KINDE pitty chokes my spleene; brave scorn forbids
Those teares to issue which swell my eye-lids,
I must not laugh, nor weepe sinnes, and be wise,
Can railing then cure these worne maladies?
Is not our Mistresse faire Religion,   5
As worthy of all our Soules devotion,
As vertue was in the first blinded age?
Are not heavens joyes as valiant to asswage
Lusts, as earths honour was to them? Alas,
As wee do them in meanes, shall they surpasse   10
Us in the end, and shall thy fathers spirit
Meete blinde Philosophers in heaven, whose merit
Of strict life may be imputed faith, and heare
Thee, whom hee taught so easie wayes and neare
To follow, damn'd? O if thou dar'st, feare this.   15
This feare great courage, and high valour is.
Dar'st thou ayd mutinous Dutch, and dar'st thou lay
Thee in ships woodden Sepulchers, a prey
To leaders rage, to stormes, to shot, to dearth?
Dar'st thou dive seas, and dungeons of the earth?   20
Hast thou couragious fire to thaw the ice
Of frozen North discoveries? and thrise
Colder then Salamanders, like divine
Children in th'oven, fires of Spaine, and the line,
Whose countries limbecks to our bodies bee,   25
Canst thou for gaine beare? and must every hee
Which cryes not, Goddesse, to thy Mistresse, draw,
Or eate thy poysonous words? courage of straw!
O desperate coward, wilt thou seeme bold, and
To thy foes and his (who made thee to stand   30

Sentinell in his worlds garrison) thus yeeld,
And for forbid warres, leave th'appointed field?
Know thy foes: The foule Devill (whom thou
Strivest to please,) for hate, not love, would allow
Thee faine, his whole Realme to be quit; and as   35
The worlds all parts wither away and passe,
So the worlds selfe, thy other lov'd foe, is
In her decrepit wayne, and thou loving this,
Dost love a withered and worne strumpet; last,
Flesh (it selfes death) and joyes which flesh can taste,   40
Thou lovest; and thy faire goodly soule, which doth
Give this flesh power to taste joy, thou dost loath.
Seeke true religion. O where? Mirreus
Thinking her unhous'd here, and fled from us,
Seekes her at Rome; there, because hee doth know   45
That shee was there a thousand yeares agoe,
He loves her ragges so, as wee here obey
The statecloth where the Prince sate yesterday.
Crates to such brave Loves will not be inthrall'd,
But loves her onely, who at Geneva is call'd   50
Religion, plaine, simple, sullen, yong,
Contemptuous, yet unhansome; As among
Lecherous humors, there is one that judges
No wenches wholsome, but course country drudges.
Graius stayes still at home here, and because   55
Some Preachers, vile ambitious bauds, and lawes
Still new like fashions, bid him thinke that shee
Which dwels with us, is onely perfect, hee
Imbraceth her, whom his Godfathers will
Tender to him, being tender, as Wards still   60
Take such wives as their Guardians offer, or
Pay valewes. Carelesse Phrygius doth abhorre
All, because all cannot be good, as one
Knowing some women whores, dares marry none.

46

Graccus loves all as one, and thinkes that so   65
As women do in divers countries goe
In divers habits, yet are still one kinde;
So doth, so is Religion; and this blind-
nesse too much light breeds; but unmoved thou
Of force must one, and forc'd but one allow;   70
And the right—aske thy father which is shee,
Let him aske his; though truth and falshood bee
Neare twins, yet truth a little elder is;
Be busie to seeke her, beleeve mee this,
Hee's not of none, nor worst, that seekes the best.   75
To adore, or scorne an image, or protest,
May all be bad; doubt wisely; in strange way
To stand inquiring right, is not to stray;
To sleepe, or runne wrong, is. On a huge hill,
Cragged, and steep, Truth stands, and hee that will   80
Reach her, about must, and about must goe;
And what the hills suddennes resists, winne so;
Yet strive so, that before age, deaths twilight,
Thy Soule rest, for none can worke in that night.
To will, implyes delay, therefore now doe: 85
Hard deeds, the bodies paines; hard knowledge too
The mindes indeavours reach, and mysteries
Are like the Sunne, dazling, yet plaine to all eyes.
Keepe the truth which thou hast found; men do not stand
In so ill case, that God hath with his hand   90
Sign'd Kings blanck-charters to kill whom they hate,
Nor are they Vicars, but hangmen to Fate.
Foole and wretch, wilt thou let thy Soule be tyed
To mans lawes, by which she shall not be tryed
At the last day? Oh, will it then boot thee   95
To say a Philip, or a Gregory,
A Harry, or a Martin taught thee this?
Is not this excuse for mere contraries,

Equally strong? cannot both sides say so?
That thou mayest rightly obey power, her bounds know; 100
Those past, her nature, and name is chang'd; to be
Then humble to her is idolatrie.
As streames are, Power is; those blest flowers that dwell
At the rough streames calme head, thrive and do well,
But having left their roots, and themselves given 105
To the streames tyrannous rage, alas, are driven
Through mills, and rockes, and woods, and at last, almost
Consum'd in going, in the sea are lost:
So perish Soules, which more chuse mens unjust
Power from God claym'd, then God himselfe to trust. 110

LETTERS TO SEVERALL
PERSONAGES

To Sʳ *Henry Goodyere*

Who makes the Past, a patterne for next yeare,
  Turnes no new leafe, but still the same things reads,
Seene things, he sees againe, heard things doth heare,
  And makes his life, but like a paire of beads.

A Palace, when 'tis that, which it should be, 5
  Leaves growing, and stands such, or else decayes:
But hee which dwels there, is not so; for hee
  Strives to urge upward, and his fortune raise;

So had your body'her morning, hath her noone,
  And shall not better; her next change is night: 10
But her faire larger guest, to'whom Sun and Moone
  Are sparkes, and short liv'd, claimes another right.

The noble Soule by age growes lustier,
   Her appetite, and her digestion mend,
Wee must not sterve, nor hope to pamper her   15
   With womens milke, and pappe unto the end.

Provide you manlyer dyet. You have seene
   All libraries, which are Schools, Camps, and Courts;
But aske your Garners if you have not beene
   In harvests, too indulgent to your sports.   20

Would you redeeme it? then your selfe transplant
   A while from hence. Perchance outlandish ground
Beares no more wit, then ours, but yet more scant
   Are those diversions there, which here abound.

To be a stranger hath that benefit,   25
   Wee can beginnings, but not habits choke.
Goe; whither? Hence; you get, if you forget;
   New faults, till they prescribe in us, are smoake.

Our sole, whose country'is heaven, and God her father,
   Into this world, corruptions sinke, is sent,   30
Yet, so much in her travaile she doth gather,
   That she returnes home, wiser then she went;

It payes you well, if it teach you to spare,
   And make you'asham'd, to make your hawks praise, yours,
Which when herselfe she lessens in the aire,   35
   You then first say, that high enough she toures.

However, keepe the lively tast you hold
   Of God, love him as now, but feare him more,
And in your afternoones thinke what you told
   And promis'd him, at morning prayer before.   40

Let falshood like a discord anger you,
   Else be not froward. But why doe I touch
Things, of which none is in your practise new,
   And Tables, or fruit-trenchers teach as much;

But thus I make you keepe your promise, Sir,   45
   Riding I had you, though you still staid there,
And in these thoughts, although you never stirre,
   You came with mee to Micham, and are here.

To Mrs *M. H.*

MAD paper stay, and grudge not here to burne
   With all those sonnes whom my braine did create,
At lest lye hid with mee, till thou returne
   To rags againe, which is thy native state.

What though thou have enough unworthinesse   5
   To come unto great place as others doe,
That's much, emboldens, pulls, thrusts I confesse,
   But 'tis not all, thou should'st be wicked too.

And, that thou canst not learne, or not of mee;
   Yet thou wilt goe. Goe, since thou goest to her   10
Who lacks but faults to be a Prince, for shee,
   Truth, whom they dare not pardon, dares preferre.

But when thou com'st to that perplexing eye
   Which equally claimes *love* and *reverence*,
Thou wilt not long dispute it, thou wilt die;   15
   And, having little now, have then no sense.

Yet when her warme redeeming hand, which is
   A miracle; and made such to worke more,
Doth touch thee (saples leafe) thou grow'st by this
   Her creature; glorify'd more then before.   20

Then as a mother which delights to heare
   Her early child mis-speake halfe uttered words,
Or, because majesty doth never feare
   Ill or bold speech, she Audience affords.

And then, cold speechlesse wretch, thou diest againe,   25
    And wisely; what discourse is left for thee?
For, speech of ill, and her, thou must abstaine,
    And is there any good which is not shee?

Yet maist thou praise her servants, though not her,
    And wit, and vertue,'and honòur her attend,   30
And since they'are but her cloathes, thou shalt not erre,
    If thou her shape and beauty'and grace commend.

Who knowes thy destiny? when thou hast done,
    Perchance her Cabinet may harbour thee,
Whither all noble ambitious wits doe runne,   35
    A nest almost as full of Good as shee.

When thou art there, if any, whom wee know,
    Were sav'd before, and did that heaven partake,
When she revolves his papers, marke what show
    Of favour, she alone to them doth make.   40

Marke, if to get them, she o'r skip the rest,
    Marke, if shee read them twice, or kisse the name;
Marke, if she doe the same that they protest,
    Marke, if she marke whether her woman came.

Marke, if slight things be'objected, and o'r blowne,   45
    Marke, if her oathes against him be not still
Reserv'd, and that shee grieves she's not her owne,
    And chides the doctrine that denies Freewill.

I bid thee not doe this to be my spie;
    Nor to make my selfe her familiar;   50
But so much I doe love her choyce, that I
    Would faine love him that shall be lov'd of her.

AN ANATOMY OF THE WORLD

From *The first Anniversary*

WHEN that rich Soule which to her heaven is gone,
Whom all do celebrate, who know they have one,
(For who is sure he hath a Soule, unlesse
It see, and judge, and follow worthinesse,
And by Deedes praise it? hee who doth not this,   5
May lodge an In-mate soule, but 'tis not his.)
When that Queene ended here her progresse time,
And, as t'her standing house to heaven did climbe,
Where loath to make the Saints attend her long,
She's now a part both of the Quire, and Song,   10
This World, in that great earthquake languished;
For in a common bath of teares it bled,
Which drew the strongest vitall spirits out:
But succour'd then with a perplexed doubt,
Whether the world did lose, or gaine in this,   15
(Because since now no other way there is,
But goodnesse, to see her, whom all would see,
All must endeavour to be good as shee,)
This great consumption to a fever turn'd,
And so the world had fits; it joy'd, it mourn'd. . . .   20

Thus man, this worlds Vice-Emperour, in whom   161
All faculties, all graces are at home;
And if in other creatures they appeare,
They're but mans Ministers, and Legats there,
To worke on their rebellions, and reduce   165
Them to Civility, and to mans use:
This man, whom God did wooe, and loth t'attend
Till man came up, did downe to man descend,

This man, so great, that all that is, is his,
Oh what a trifle, and poore thing he is!   170
If man were any thing, he's nothing now:
Helpe, or at least some time to wast, allow
T'his other wants, yet when he did depart
With her whom we lament, hee lost his heart.
She, of whom th'Ancients seem'd to prophesie,   175
When they call'd vertues by the name of *shee*;
Shee in whom vertue was so much refin'd,
That for Allay unto so pure a minde
Shee tooke the weaker Sex; shee that could drive
The poysonous tincture, and the staine of *Eve*,   180
Out of her thoughts, and deeds; and purifie
All, by a true religious Alchymie;
Shee, shee is dead; shee's dead: when thou knowest
    this,
Thou knowest how poore a trifling thing man is. . . .

This is the worlds condition now, and now   219
She that should all parts to reunion bow,
She that had all Magnetique force alone,
To draw, and fasten sundred parts in one;
She whom wise nature had invented then
When she observ'd that every sort of men
Did in their voyage in this worlds Sea stray,   225
And needed a new compasse for their way;
She that was best, and first originall
Of all faire copies, and the generall
Steward to Fate; she whose rich eyes, and brest
Guilt the West Indies, and perfum'd the East;   230
Whose having breath'd in this world, did bestow
Spice on those Iles, and bad them still smell so,
And that rich Indie which doth gold interre,
Is but as single money, coyn'd from her:

She to whom this world must it selfe refer,   235
As Suburbs, or the Microcosme of her,
She, shee is dead; shee's dead: when thou knowst this,
Thou knowst how lame a cripple this world is. . . .

And, Oh, it can no more be questioned   305
That beauties best, proportion, is dead,
Since even griefe it selfe, which now alone
Is left us, is without proportion.
Shee by whose lines proportion should bee
Examin'd, measure of all Symmetree,   310
Whom had that Ancient seen, who thought soules made
Of Harmony, he would at next have said
That Harmony was shee, and thence infer,
That soules were but Resultances from her,
And did from her into our bodies goe,   315
As to our eyes, the formes from objects flow:
Shee, who if those great Doctors truly said
That the Arke to mans proportions was made,
Had been a type for that, as that might be
A type of her in this, that contrary   320
Both Elements, and Passions liv'd at peace
In her, who caus'd all Civill war to cease.
Shee, after whom, what forme fo'er we see,
Is discord, and rude incongruitie;
Shee, shee is dead, shee's dead; when thou knowst this 325
Thou knowst how ugly a monster this world is: . . .

Here therefore be the end: And, blessed maid,   443
Of whom is meant what ever hath been said,
Or shall be spoken well by any tongue,   445
Whose name refines course lines, and makes prose song,
Accept this tribute, and his first yeares rent,
Who till his darke short tapers end be spent,

As oft as thy feast sees this widowed earth,
Will yearely celebrate thy second birth,   450
That is, thy death; for though the soule of man
Be got when man is made, 'tis borne but than
When man doth die; our body's as the wombe,
And, as a Mid-wife, death directs it home.
And you her creatures, whom she workes upon,   455
And have your last, and best concoction
From her example, and her vertue, if you
In reverence to her, do thinke it due,
That no one should her praises thus rehearse,
As matter fit for Chronicle, not verse;   460
Vouchsafe to call to minde that God did make
A last, and lasting'st peece, a song. He spake
To *Moses* to deliver unto all,
That song, because hee knew they would let fall
The Law, the Prophets, and the History,   465
But keepe the song still in their memory:
Such an opinion (in due measure) made
Me this great Office boldly to invade:
Nor could incomprehensiblenesse deterre
Mee, from thus trying to emprison her,   470
Which when I saw that a strict grave could doe,
I saw not why verse might not do so too.

From *The second Anniversary*

NOTHING could make me sooner to confesse
That this world had an everlastingnesse,
Then to consider, that a yeare is runne,
Since both this lower world's, and the Sunnes Sunne,
The Lustre, and the vigor of this All,   5
Did set; 'twere blasphemie to say, did fall.

But as a ship which hath strooke saile, doth runne
By force of that force which before, it wonne: . . .
Or as a Lute, which in moist weather, rings   19
Her knell alone, by cracking of her strings:
So struggles this dead world, now shee is gone;
For there is motion in corruption.
As some daies are at the Creation nam'd,
Before the Sunne, the which fram'd daies, was fram'd,
So after this Sunne's set, some shew appeares,   25
And orderly vicissitude of yeares.
Yet a new Deluge, and of *Lethe* flood,
Hath drown'd us all, All have forgot all good,
Forgetting her, the maine reserve of all.
Yet in this deluge, grosse and generall,   30
Thou seest me strive for life; my life shall bee,
To be hereafter prais'd, for praysing thee;
Immortall Maid, who though thou would'st refuse
The name of Mother, be unto my Muse
A Father, since her chast Ambition is,   35
Yearely to bring forth such a child as this.
These Hymnes may worke on future wits, and so
May great Grand children of thy prayses grow,
And so, though not revive, embalme and spice
The world, which else would putrifie with vice.   40
For thus, Man may extend thy progeny,
Untill man doe but vanish, and not die.
These Hymnes thy issue, may encrease so long,
As till Gods great *Venite* change the song.
Thirst for that time, O my insatiate soule,   45
And serve thy thirst, with Gods safe-sealing Bowle.
Be thirstie still, and drinke still till thou goe
To th'only Health, to be Hydroptique so.
Forget this rotten world; And unto thee
Let thine owne times as an old storie bee.   50

Be not concern'd: studie not why, nor when;
Doe not so much as not beleeve a man.
For though to erre, be worst, to try truths forth,
Is far more business, then this world is worth. . . .
Look upward; that's towards her, whose happy state   65
We now lament not, but congratulate.
Shee, to whom all this world was but a stage,
Where all sat harkning how her youthfull age
Should be emploi'd, because in all shee did,
Some Figure of the Golden times was hid.   70
Who could not lacke, what e'r this world could give,
Because shee was the forme, that made it live;
Nor could complaine, that this world was unfit
To be staid in, then when shee was in it;
Shee that first tried indifferent desires   75
By vertue, and vertue by religious fires,
Shee to whose person Paradise adher'd,
As Courts to Princes, shee whose eyes ensphear'd
Star-light enough, t'have made the South controule,
(Had shee beene there) she Star-full Northerne Pole,   80
Shee, shee is gone; she is gone; when thou knowest this,
What fragmentary rubbidge this world is
Thou knowest, and that it is not worth a thought;
He honors it too much that thinkes it nought.
Thinke then, my soule, that death is but a Groome,   85
Which brings a Taper to the outward roome,
Whence thou spiest first a little glimmering light,
And after brings it nearer to thy sight:
For such approaches doth heaven make in death.
Thinke thy selfe labouring now with broken breath,   90
And thinke those broken and soft Notes to bee
Division, and thy happyest Harmonie.
Thinke thee laid on thy death-bed, loose and slacke;
And thinke that, but unbinding of a packe,

To take one precious thing, thy soule from thence.   95
Thinke thy selfe parch'd with fevers violence,
Anger thine ague more, by calling it
Thy Physicke; chide the slacknesse of the fit.
Thinke that thou hear'st thy knell, and think no more,
But that, as Bels cal'd thee to Church before,   100
So this, to the Triumphant Church, calls thee.
Thinke Satans Sergeants round about thee bee,
And thinke that but for Legacies they thrust;
Give one thy Pride, to'another give thy Lust:
Give them those sinnes which they gave thee before,   105
And trust th'immaculate blood to wash thy score.
Thinke thy friends weeping round, and thinke that they
Weepe but because they goe not yet thy way.
Thinke that they close thine eyes, and thinke in this,
That they confesse much in the world, amisse,   110
Who dare not trust a dead mans eye with that,
Which they from God, and Angels cover not.
Thinke that they shroud thee up, and think from thence
They reinvest thee in white innocence.
Thinke that thy body rots, and (if so low,   115
Thy soule exalted so, thy thoughts can goe,)
Think thee a Prince, who of themselves create
Wormes which insensibly devoure their State.
Thinke that they bury thee, and thinke that right
Laies thee to sleepe but a Saint Lucies night. . . .   120

Thou look'st through spectacles; small things seeme great 293
Below; But up unto the watch-towre get,
And see all things despoyl'd of fallacies:
Thou shalt not peepe through lattices of eyes,
Nor heare through Labyrinths of eares, nor learne
By circuit, or collections to discerne.

In heaven thou straight know'st all, concerning it,
And what concernes it not, shalt straight forget.   300
There thou (but in no other schoole) maist bee
Perchance, as learned, and as full, as shee,
Shee who all libraries had throughly read
At home in her owne thoughts, and practised
So much good as would make as many more: 305
Shee whose example they must all implore,
Who would or doe, or thinke well, and confesse
That all the vertuous Actions they expresse,
Are but a new, and worse edition
Of her some one thought, or one action: 310
She who in th'art of knowing Heaven, was growne
Here upon earth, to such perfection,
That she hath, ever since to Heaven she came,
(In a far fairer print,) but read the same:
Shee, shee not satisfied with all this waight,   315
(For so much knowledge, as would over-fraight
Another, did but ballast her) is gone
As well t'enjoy, as get perfection.
And cals us after her, in that shee tooke,
(Taking her selfe) our best, and worthiest booke. . . .   320

And she made peace, for no peace is like this,   363
That beauty, and chastity together kisse: . . .   364

And what essentiall joy can'st thou expect   387
Here upon earth? what permanent effect
Of transitory causes? Dost thou love
Beauty? (And beauty worthy'st is to move)   390
Poore cousened cousenor, *that* she, and *that* thou,
Which did begin to love, are neither now;
You are both fluid, chang'd since yesterday;
Next day repaires, (but ill) last dayes decay.

Nor are, (although the river keepe the name)   395
Yesterdaies waters, and to daies the same.
So flowes her face, and thine eyes, neither now
That Saint, nor Pilgrime, which your loving vow
Concern'd, remaines; but whil'st you thinke you bee
Constant, you'are hourely in inconstancie. . . .   400

So much mankinde true happinesse mistakes;   433
No Joy enjoyes that man, that many makes.
Then, Soule, to thy first pitch worke up againe;   435
Know that all lines which circles doe containe,
For once that they the Center touch, doe touch
Twice the circumference; and be thou such;
Double on heaven thy thoughts on earth emploid;
All will not serve; Only who have enjoy'd   440
The sight of God, in fulnesse, can thinke it;
For it is both the object, and the wit.
This is essentiall joy, where neither hee
Can suffer diminution, nor wee;
'Tis such a full, and such a filling good;   445
Had th'Angels once look'd on him, they had stood.
To fill the place of one of them, or more,
Shee whom wee celebrate, is gone before.
She, who had Here so much essentiall joy,
As no chance could distract, much lesse destroy;   450
Who with God's presence was acquainted so,
(Hearing, and speaking to him) as to know
His face in any naturall Stone, or Tree,
Better then when in Images they be:
Who kept by diligent devotion,   455
Gods Image, in such reparation,
Within her heart, that what decay was growne,
Was her first Parents fault, and not her owne:

Who being solicited to any act,
Still heard God pleading his safe precontract;   460
Who by a faithfull confidence, was here
Betroth'd to God, and now is married there;
Whose twilights were more cleare, then our mid-day;
Who dreamt devoutlier, then most use to pray;
Who being here fil'd with grace, yet strove to bee,   465
Both where more grace, and more capacitie
At once is given: she to Heaven is gone,
Who made this world in some proportion
A heaven, and here, became unto us all,
Joy, (as our joyes admit) essentiall.   470
But could this low world joyes essentiall touch,
Heavens accidentall joyes would passe them much.

EPICEDES AND OBSEQUIES

From *Elegie on M^{ris} Boulstred*

O STRONG and long-liv'd death, how cam'st thou in?   21
    And how without Creation didst begin?
Thou hast, and shalt see dead, before thou dyest,
    All the foure Monarchies, and Antichrist.
How could I thinke thee nothing, that see now   25
    In all this All, nothing else is, but thou.
Our births, and lives, vices, and vertues, bee
    Wastfull consumptions, and degrees of thee. . . .
And though thou beest, O mighty bird of prey,   31
    So much reclaim'd by God, that thou must lay
All that thou kill'st at his feet, yet doth hee
    Reserve but few, and leaves the most to thee.
And of those few, now thou hast overthrowne   35
    One whom thy blow makes, not ours, nor thine own.

She was more stories high: hopelesse to come
    To her Soule, thou'hast offer'd at her lower roome.
Her Soule and body was a King and Court:
    But thou hast both of Captaine mist and fort.   40
As houses fall not, though the King remove,
    Bodies of Saints rest for their soules above.
Death gets 'twixt soules and bodies such a place
As sinne insinuates 'twixt just men and grace,
Both worke a separation, no divorce.   45
    Her Soule is gone to usher up her corse,
Which shall be'almost another soule, for there
    Bodies are purer, then best Soules are here.
Because in her, her virtues did outgoe
    Her yeares, would'st thou, O emulous death, do so?   50
And kill her young to thy losse? must the cost
    Of beauty,'and wit, apt to doe harme, be lost?
What though thou found'st her proofe'gainst sins of
       youth?
    Oh, every age a diverse sinne pursueth.
Thou should'st have stay'd, and taken better hold,   55
    Shortly, ambitious; covetous, when old,
She might have prov'd: and such devotion
    Might once have stray'd to superstition.
If all her vertues must have growne, yet might
    Abundant virtue'have bred a proud delight.   60
Had she persever'd just, there would have bin
    Some that would sinne, mis-thinking she did sinne.
Such as would call her friendship, love, and faine
    To sociablenesse, a name profane;
Or sinne, by tempting, or, not daring that,   65
    By wishing, though they never told her what.
Thus might'st thou'have slain more soules, had'st thou not
       crost
    Thy selfe, and to triumph, thine army lost.

Yet though these wayes be lost, thou has left one,
Which is, immoderate griefe that she is gone. 70
But we may scape that sinne, yet weepe as much,
Our teares are due, because we are not such.
Some teares, that knot of friends, her death must cost,
Because the chaine is broke, though no linke lost.

From *Elegie on the L. C.*

HERE needs no marble Tombe, since hee is gone,
He, and about him, his, are turn'd to stone.

From THE PROGRESSE OF THE SOULE

IV

GREAT Destiny the Commissary of God,
That hast mark'd out a path and period
For every thing; who, where wee of-spring tooke,
Our wayes and ends seest at one instant; Thou
Knot of all causes, thou whose changelesse brow 35
Ne'r smiles nor frownes, O vouch thou safe to looke
And shew my story, in thy eternall booke:
That (if my prayer be fit) I may'understand
So much my selfe, as to know with what hand,
How scant, or liberall this my lifes race is spand. 40

V

To my sixe lustres almost now outwore,
Except thy booke owe mee so many more,
Except my legend be free from the letts
Of steepe ambition, sleepie povertie,
Spirit-quenching sicknesse, dull captivitie, 45

Distracting businesse, and from beauties nets,
And all that calls from this, and to others whets,
O let me not launch out, but let mee save
Th'expense of braine and spirit; that my grave
His right and due, a whole unwasted man may have.　　50

VI

But if my dayes be long, and good enough,
In vaine this sea shall enlarge, or enrough
It selfe; for I will through the wave, and fome,
And shall, in sad lone wayes a lively spright,
Make my darke heavy Poëm light, and light.　　55
For though through many streights, and lands I roame,
I launch at paradise, and I saile towards home;
The course I there began, shall here be staid,
Sailes hoised there, stroke here, and anchors laid
In Thames, which were at Tigrys, and Euphrates waide.　60

VII

For the great soule which here amongst us now
Doth dwell, and moves that hand, and tongue, and brow,
Which, as the Moone the sea, moves us; to heare
Whose story, with long patience you will long;
(For 'tis the crowne, and last straine of my song)　　65
This soule to whom *Luther*, and *Mahomet* were
Prisons of flesh; this soule which oft did teare,
And mend the wracks of th'Empire, and late Rome,
And liv'd when every great change did come,
Had first in paradise, a low, but fatall roome.　　70

VIII

Yet no low roome, nor then the greatest, lesse,
If (as devout and sharpe men fitly guesse)
That Crosse, our joy, and griefe, where nailes did tye

That All, which alwayes was all, every where;
Which could not sinne, and yet all sinnes did beare;   75
Which could not die, yet could not chuse but die;
Stood in the selfe same roome in Calvarie,
Where first grew the forbidden learned tree,
For on that tree hung in security
   This Soule, made by the Makers will from pulling free. 80

IX

Prince of the orchard, faire as dawning morne,
Fenc'd with the law, and ripe as soone as borne
That apple grew, which this Soule did enlive,
Till the then climing serpent, that now creeps
For that offence, for which all mankinde weepes,   85
Tooke it, and t'her whom the first man did wive
(Whom and her race, only forbiddings drive)
He gave it, she t'her husband, both did eate;
So perished the eaters, and the meate:
   And wee (for treason taints the blood) thence die and
     sweat.
                                90

X

Man all at once was there by woman slaine,
And one by one we'are here slaine o'er againe
By them. The mother poison'd the well-head,
The daughters here corrupt us, Rivolets;
No smalnesse scapes, no greatnesse breaks their nets;   95
She thrust us out, and by them we are led
Astray, from turning, to whence we are fled.
Were prisoners Judges, 'twould seeme rigorous,
Shee sinn'd, we beare; part of our paine is, thus
   To love them, whose fault to this painfull love yoak'd
     us.
                                100

DIVINE POEMS

Holy Sonnets

I

Thou hast made me, And shall thy worke decay?
Repaire me now, for now mine end doth haste,
I runne to death, and death meets me as fast,
And all my pleasures are like yesterday;
I dare not move my dimme eyes any way,　　　　5
Despaire behind, and death before doth cast
Such terrour, and my feeble flesh doth waste
By sinne in it, which it t'wards hell doth weigh;
Onely thou art above, and when towards thee
By thy leave I can looke, I rise againe;　　　　10
But our old subtle foe so tempteth me,
That not one houre my selfe I can sustaine;
Thy Grace may wing me to prevent his art,
And thou like Adamant draw mine iron heart.

VII

At the round earths imagin'd corners, blow
Your trumpets, Angells, and arise, arise
From death, you numberlesse infinities
Of soules, and to your scattered bodies goe,
All whom the flood did, and fire shall o'erthrow,　　　　5
All whom warre, dearth, age, agues, tyrannies,
Despaire, law, chance, hath slaine, and you whose eyes
Shall behold God, and never tast deaths woe.
But let them sleepe, Lord, and mee mourne a space,
For, if above all these, my sinnes abound,　　　　10
'Tis late to aske abundance of thy grace,
When wee are there; here on this lowly ground,
Teach mee how to repent; for that's as good
As if thou'hadst seal'd my pardon, with thy blood.

X

DEATH be not proud, though some have called thee
Mighty and dreadfull, for, thou art not soe,
For, those, whom thou think'st, thou dost overthrow,
Die not, poore death, nor yet canst thou kill mee.
From rest and sleepe, which but thy pictures bee,⠀⠀⠀⠀5
Much pleasure, then from thee, much more must flow,
And soonest our best men with thee doe goe,
Rest of their bones, and soules deliverie.
Thou art slave to Fate, chance, kings, and desperate men,
And dost with poyson, warre, and sicknesse dwell,⠀⠀⠀10
And poppie, or charmes can make us sleepe as well,
And better then thy stroake; why swell'st thou then?
One short sleepe past, wee wake eternally,
And death shall be no more; death, thou shalt die.

SPIT in my face you Jewes, and pierce my side,
Buffet, and scoffe, scourge, and crucifie mee,
For I have sinn'd, and sinn'd, and onely hee,
Who could do no iniquitie, hath dyed:
But by my death can not be satisfied⠀⠀⠀⠀5
My sinnes, which passe the Jewes impiety:
They kill'd once an inglorious man, but I
Crucifie him daily, being now glorified.
Oh let mee then, his strange love still admire:
Kings pardon, but he bore our punishment.⠀⠀⠀10
And *Jacob* came cloth'd in vile harsh attire
But to supplant, and with gainfull intent:
God cloth'd himselfe in vile mans flesh, that so
Hee might be weake enough to suffer woe.

XIV

BATTER my heart, three person'd God; for, you
As yet but knocke, breathe, shine, and seeke to mend;
That I may rise, and stand, o'erthrow mee,'and bend
Your force, to breake, blowe, burn and make me new.
I, like an usurpt towne, to'another due,   5
Labour to'admit you, but Oh, to no end,
Reason your viceroy in mee, mee should defend,
But is captiv'd, and proves weake or untrue.
Yet dearely'I love you,'and would be loved faine,
But am betroth'd unto your enemie: 10
Divorce mee,'untie, or breake that knot againe,
Take mee to you, imprison mee, for I
Except you'enthrall mee, never shall be free,
Nor ever chast, except you ravish mee.

XVIII

SHOW me deare Christ, thy spouse, so bright and clear.
What! is it She, which on the other shore
Goes richly painted? or which rob'd and tore
Laments and mournes in Germany and here?
Sleepes she a thousand, then peepes up one yeare?   5
Is she selfe truth and errs? now new, now outwore?
Doth she, and did she, and shall she evermore
On one, on seaven, or on no hill appeare?
Dwells she with us, or like adventuring knights
First travaile we to seeke and then make Love?   10
Betray kind husband thy spouse to our sights,
And let myne amorous sole court thy mild Dove,
Who is most trew, and pleasing to thee, then
When she'is embrac'd and open to most men.

From *The Litanie*

WHEN wee are mov'd to seeme religious   188
Only to vent wit, Lord deliver us.   189

A sinner is more musique, when he prayes,   200
    Then spheares, or Angels praises bee.   201

Hymne to God my God, in my sicknesse

SINCE I am comming to that Holy roome,
    Where, with thy Quire of Saints for evermore,
I shall be made thy Musique; As I come
    I tune my Instrument here at the dore,
    And what I must doe then, thinke here before.   5

Whilst my Physitians by their love are growne
    Cosmographers, and I their Mapp, who lie
Flat on this bed, that by them may be showne
    That this is my South-west discoverie
    Per fretum febris, by these streights to die,   10

I joy, that in these straits, I see my West;
    For, though theire currants yeeld returne to none,
What shall my West hurt me? As West and East
    In all flatt Maps (and I am one) are one,
    So death doth touch the Resurrection.   15

Is the Pacifique Sea my home? Or are
    The Easterne riches? Is *Jerusalem*?
Anyan, and *Magellan*, and *Gibraltare*,
    All streights, and none but streights, are wayes to them,
    Whether where *Japhet* dwelt, or *Cham*, or *Sem*.   20

We thinke that *Paradise* and *Calvarie*,
   Christs Crosse, and *Adams* tree, stood in one place;
Looke Lord, and finde both *Adams* met in me;
   As the first *Adams* sweat surrounds my face,
   May the last *Adams* blood my soule embrace.   25

So, in his purple wrapp'd receive mee Lord,
   By these his thornes give me his other Crowne;
And as to others soules I preach'd thy word,
   Be this my Text, my Sermon to mine owne,
   Therfore that he may raise the Lord throws down.   30

Preface to BIATHANATOS

Declaring the Reasons, the Purpose, the way, and
the end of the author

BEZA, a man as eminent and illustrious, in the full glory
and Noone of Learning, as others were in the dawning, and
Morning, when any, the least sparkle was notorious, confesseth of himself, that only for the anguish of a Scurffe,
which over-ranne his head, he had once drown'd himselfe
from the Miller's bridge in Paris, if his Uncle by chance had
not then come that way; I have often such a sickely inclination. And, whether it be, because I had my first breeding
and conversation with men of a suppressed and afflicted
10 Religion, accustomed to the despite of death, and hungry
of an imagin'd Martyrdome; Or that the common Enemie
find that doore worst locked against him in mee; Or that
there bee a perplexitie and flexibility in the doctrine it selfe;
Or because my Conscience ever assures me, that no rebellious
grudging at Gods gifts, nor other sinfull concurrence accom-
panies these thoughts in me, or that a brave scorn, or that a
faint cowardlinesse beget it, whensoever any affliction assails
me, mee thinks I have the keyes of my prison in mine owne
hand, and no remedy presents it selfe so soone to my heart,
20 as mine own sword. Often Meditation of this hath wonne
me to a charitable interpretation of their action, who dy so:
and provoked me a little to watch and exagitate their
reasons, which pronounce so peremptory judgements upon
them.

A devout and godly man, hath guided us well, and rectified
our uncharitablenesse in such cases, by this remembrance,
[Scis lapsum etc. *Thou knowest this mans fall, but thou*
knowest not his wrastling; which perchance was such, that

almost his very fall is justified and accepted of God.] For, to
this end, saith one, [*God hath appointed us tentations, that
we might have some excuses for our sinnes, when he calls us to
account.*]

An uncharitable mis-interpreter unthriftily demolishes
his own house, and repaires not another. He loseth without
any gaine or profit to any. And, as Tertullian comparing
and making equall, him which provokes another, and him
who will be provoked by another, says, [*There is no difference, but that the provoker offended first, And that is nothing,* 10
because in evill there is no respect of Order or Prioritie.] So
wee may soone become as ill as any offendor, if we offend
in a severe increpation of the fact. For, Climachus in his
Ladder of Paradise, places these two steps very neere one
another, when hee sayes, [*Though in the world it were possible
for thee, to escape all defiling by actuall sinne, yet by judging
and condemning those who are defiled, thou art defiled.*] In
this thou art defiled, as *Basil* notes, [*That in comparing
others sinnes, thou canst not avoid excusing thine owne*]
Especially this is done, if thy zeale be too fervent in the 20
reprehension of others: For, as in most other Accidents, so
in this also, Sinne hath the nature of Poyson, that [*It enters
easiest, and works fastest upon cholerique constitutions.*] It is
good counsell of the Pharises stiled, [*Ne judices proximum,
donec ad ejus locum pertingas.*] Feele and wrastle with such
tentations as he hath done, and thy zeale will be tamer.
For, [*Therefore* (saith the Apostle) *it became Christ to be like
us, that he might be mercifull.*]

If therefore after a Christian protestation of an innocent
purpose herein, And after a submission of all which is said, 30
not only to every Christian Church, but to every Christian
man, and after an entreaty, that the Reader will follow this
advice of Tabaeus, [*Qui litigant, sint ambo in conspectu tuo
mali et rei,*] and trust neither me, nor the adverse part, but

the Reasons, there be any scandall in this enterprise of mine, it is Taken, not Given. And though I know, that the malitious prejudged man, and the lazy affectors of ignorance, will use the same calumnies and obtrectations toward me, (for the voyce and sound of the Snake and Goose is all one) yet because I thought, that as in the poole of *Bethsaida*, there was no health till the water was troubled, so the best way to finde the truth in this matter, was to debate and vexe it, (for [*We must as well dispute* de veritate, *as* pro veritate,]) I
10 abstained not for feare of mis-interpretation from this undertaking. Our stomachs are not now so tender, and queasie, after so long feeding upon solid Divinity, nor we so umbragious and startling, having been so long enlightened in Gods path, that wee should thinke any truth strange to us, or relapse into that childish age, in which a Councell in France forbad *Aristotles Metaphysiques*, and punished with Excommunication the excribing, reading, or having that booke.

Contemplative and bookish men, must of necessitie be more quarrelsome than others, because they contend not
20 about matter of fact, nor can determine their controversies by any certaine witnesses, nor judges. But as long as they goe towards peace, that is Truth, it is no matter which way. The tutelare Angels resisted one another in *Persia*, but neither resisted Gods revealed purpose. *Hierome* and *Gregorie* seem to be of opinion, that *Salomon* is damned; *Ambrose* and *Augustine*, that he is saved: All Fathers, all zealous of Gods glory. At the same time when the *Romane* Church canonized *Becket*, the Schooles of *Paris* disputed whether hee could be saved; both Catholique Judges, and
30 of reverend authoritie. And after so many Ages of a devout and religious celebrating the memory of Saint *Hierome*, *Causaeus* hath spoken so dangerously, that *Campian* saies, hee pronounceth him to be as deepe in hell as the Devill. But in all such intricacies, where both opinions seem equally

to conduce to the honor of God, his Justice being as much
advanced in the one, as his Mercie in the other, it seemes
reasonable to me, that this turne the scales, if on either side
there appeare charity towards the poore soule departed. The
Church in her Hymnes and Antiphones, doth often salute
the Nayles and Crosse, with Epithets of sweetnesse, and
thanks; But the Speare which pierced Christ when he was
dead, it ever calles, *dirum Mucronem.*

This pietie, I protest againe, urges me in this discourse;
and what infirmity soever my reasons may have, yet I have
comfort in *Trismegistus* Axiome, [*Qui pius est, summè
Philosophatur.*] And therefore without any disguising, or
curious and libellous concealing, I present and object it, to
all of candour, and indifferencie, to escape that just taxation,
[*Novum malitiae genus est, et intemperantis, scribere quod
occultes.*] For as, when *Ladislaus* tooke occasion of the great
schisme, to corrupt the Nobility in Rome, and hoped thereby
to possesse the towne, to their seven Governours whom they
called *Sapientes*, they added three more, whom they called
Bonos, and confided in them; So doe I wish, and as much as
I can, effect, that to those many learned and subtile men
which have travelled in this point, some charitable and
compassionate men might be added.

If therefore, of Readers, which *Gorionides* observes to
be of foure sorts, (Spunges which attract all without dis-
tinguishing; Howre-glasses, which receive and powre out
as fast; Bagges which retaine onely the dregges of the
Spices, and let the Wine escape; And Sives, which retaine
the best onely), I finde some of the last sort, I doubt not
but they may bee hereby enlightened. And as the eyes
of *Eve*, were opened by the taste of the Apple, though it
bee said before that shee saw the beauty of the tree, So
the digesting of this may, though not present faire objects,
yet bring them to see the nakednesse and deformity of

their owne reasons, founded upon a rigorous suspition, and winne them to be of that temper, which *Chrisostome* commends, [*He which suspects benignly would faine be deceived, and bee overcome, and is piously glad, when he findes it to be false, which he did uncharitably suspect.*] And it may have as much vigour (as one observes of another Author) as the Sunne in March; it may stirre and dissolve humors, though not expell them; for that must bee a worke of a stronger power.

Every branch which is excerpted from other authors, and
10 engrafted here, is not written for the readers faith, but for illustration and comparison. Because I undertooke the declaration of such a proposition as was controverted by many, and therefore was drawne to the citation of many authorities, I was willing to goe all the way with company, and to take light from others, as well in the journey as at the journeys end. If therefore in multiplicity of not necessary citations there appeare vanity, or ostentation, or digression my honesty must make my excuse and compensation, who acknowledge as Pliny doth [*That to chuse rather to be*
20 *taken in a theft, then to give every man due,* is obnoxii animi, et infelicis ingenii.] I did it the rather because scholastique and artificiall men use this way of instructing; and I made account that I was to deal with such, because I presume that naturall men are at least enough inclinable of themselves to this doctrine.

This my way; and my end is to remove scandall. For certainly God often punisheth a sinner much more severely, because others have taken occasion of sinning by his fact. If therefore wee did correct in our selves this easines of being
30 scandalized, how much easier and lighter might we make the punishment of many transgressors? for God in his judgements hath almost made us his assistants, and counsellers, how far he shall punish; and our interpretation of anothers sinne doth often give the measure to Gods Justice or Mercy.

If therefore, since [*disorderly long haire which was pride and wantonnesse in* Absolon, *and squallor and horridnes in* Nebuchodonozor *was vertue and strength in* Samson, *and sanctification in* Samuel,] these severe men will not allow to indifferent things the best construction they are capable of, nor pardon my inclination to do so, they shall pardon me this opinion, that their severity proceeds from a self-guiltines, and give me leave to apply that of *Ennodius*, [*That it is the nature of stiffe wickednesse, to think that of others, which themselves deserve and it is all the comfort the guilty have, not to find any innocent.*]

A DEFENCE OF WOMEN'S INCONSTANCY

Juvenilia, or certaine Paradoxes and Problemes, 1633, i

THAT Women are *Inconstant*, I with any man confess, but that *Inconstancy* is a bad quality, I against any man will maintain: For every thing as it is one better than another, so is it fuller of *change*; The *Heavens* themselves continually turne, the *Starres* move, the *Moone* changeth; *Fire* whirleth, *Aire* flyeth, *Water* ebbs and flowes, the face of the *Earth* altereth her looks, *time* staies not; the Colour that is most light will take most dyes: soe in Men, they that have the most reason are the most alterable in their designes, and the darkest or most ignorant, do seldomest change; therefore Women changing more than Men, have also more *Reason*. They cannot be immutable like stockes, like stones, like the Earths dull Center; Gold that lyeth still, rusteth; Water, corrupteth; Aire that moveth not, poysoneth; then why should that which is the perfection of other things, be imputed to Women as greatest imperfection? Because thereby they deceive Men. Are not your wits pleased with those

jests, which coozen your expectation? You can call it pleasure
to be beguild in troubles, and in the most excellent toy in
the world, you call it Treacherie: I would you had your
Mistresses so constant, that they would never change, no
not so much as their *smocks*, then should you see what
sluttish vertue, *Constancy* were. *Inconstancy* is a most com-
mendable and cleanly quality, and Women in this quality
are farre more absolute than the Heavens, than the Stars,
Moone, or anything beneath it; for long observation hath
10 pickt certainty out of their mutability. The Learned are so
well acquainted with the Starrs, Signes and Planets, that
they make them but Characters, to read the meaning of the
Heaven in his own forehead. Every simple fellow can be-
speake the change of the *Moone* a great while beforehand:
but I would fain have the learnedst man so skilfull, as to
tell when the simplest Woman meaneth to varie. Learning
affords no rules to know, much less knowledge to rule the
minde of a Woman: For as *Philosophy* teacheth us, that
Light things do alwayes tend upwards, and *heavy things decline
20 downward*; Experience teacheth us otherwise, that the disposition of a *Light* Woman, is to fall down, the nature of
Women being contrary to all Art and Nature. Women are
like *Flies*, which feed among us at our Table, or *Fleas* suck-
ing our very blood, who leave not our most retired places
free from their familiarity, yet for all their fellowship will
they never be tamed or commanded by us. Women are like
the *Sun*, which is violently carried one way, yet hath a
proper course contrary; so though they, by the mastery
of some over-ruling churlish husbands, are forced to his
30 Byas, yet have they a motion of their own, which their
husbands never know of: It is the nature of nice and fastidious
mindes to know things onely to be weary of them; Women
by their slye *changeableness*, and pleasing doubleness, prevent even the mislike of those, for they can never be so well

knowne, but that there is still more unknowne. Every woman
is a *Science*; for he that plods upon a woman all his life long,
shall at length finde himselfe short of the knowledge of her:
they are borne to take down the pride of wit, and Ambition
of wisdome, making *fooles* wise in the adventuring to winne
them, *wisemen* fooles in conceit of losing their labours; *witty*
men stark mad, being confounded with their uncertainties.
Philosophers write against them for spight, not desert, that
having attained to some knowledge in all other things, in
them onely they know nothing, but are meerly ignorant: 10
Active and *Experienced* men rail against them, because they
love in their liveless and decrepit age, when all goodnesse
leaves them. These envious *Libellers* ballad against them,
because having nothing in themselves able to deserve their
love, they maliciously discommend all they cannot obtaine,
thinking to make men beleeve they know much, because
they are able to dispraise much, and rage against *Inconstancy*, when they were never admitted into so much favour
as to bee forsaken. In mine Opinion such men are happie
that Women are *Inconstant*, for so may they chance to be 20
beloved of some excellent Women (when it comes to their
turne) out of their *Inconstancy*, and mutability, though not
out of their owne desert. And what reason is there to clog
any Woman with one Man, be he never so singular? Women
had rather, and it is farre better and more Judicial to enjoy
all the vertues in several men, than but some of them in one,
for otherwise they lose their taste, like diverse sorts of meate
minced together in one dish: and to have all excellencies
in one Man (if it were possible) is *Confusion* and *Diversity*.
Now who can deny, but such as are obstinately bent to 30
undervalue their worth, are those who have not soul enough
to comprehend their excellency, Women being the most
excellent Creatures, in that Man is able to subject all things
else, and to grow wise in everything, but still persists a foole

in Woman? The greatest *Scholler*, if he once take a wife, is
found so unlearned, that he must begin his *Horne-booke*,
and all is by *Inconstancy*. To conclude therefore; this name
of *Inconstancy*, which hath so much been poisoned with
slaunders, ought to be changed into *variety*, for the which
the world is so delightfull, and a Woman for that the most
delightfull thing in this world.

LETTERS

1. *Donne's earliest extant letter*

Written from Plymouth

THE first act of that play which I said I would go over the
10 water to see is done and yet the people hisse. How it will
end I know not ast ego vicissim risero. It is true that Jonas
was in a whales belly three dayes but hee came not voluntary
as I did nor was troubled with the stinke of 150 land soldiers
as wee; & I was there 20 dayes of so very very bad wether
that even some of the marriners have been drawen to thinke
it were not altogether amisse to pray & my self heard one
of them say god help us. For all our paynes wee have seene
the land of promise Spaine. Whether wee shall enter or no
I guess not. I think there is a blott in there tables. But
20 perchaunce tis not on our dice to hitt it. Wee are now againe
at Plymouth quasi ply-mouth; for wee do nothing but eate
& scarce that: I think when wee came in the burghers tooke
us for the Spanish fleet for they have either hid or convayd
all there mony. Never was extreame beggery so extreamely
brave except when a company of mummers had lost theire
box. I do not think that 77 Kelleys could distill 10^1 out
of all the towne. He that hath supt and hath 2 or 3^8 is a
king; for none hath a crowne. Fayth, lands jerkins knight-
hoods are reprobate pawnes and but for the much gay

cloathes (which yet are much melted) I should thinke wee
were in Utopia: all are so utterly coyneles. In one bad bare
word the want is so generall that the lord generall wants,
and till this day wee wanted the lord generall: you will
pardone me if I write nothing ernest. Salute all whom thou
lovest in my name & love me as I would deserve.

2. *To my honoured friend G. G., Esquire*

[on the interpretation of the *Anniversaries*]

Sir,

   Neither your Letters, nor silence, needs excuse; your
friendship is to me an abundant possession, though you
remember me but twice in a year: He that would have two
harvests in that time, might justly value his land at a high
rate; but, Sir, as we doe not onely then thank our land,
when we gather the fruit, but acknowledge that all the year
she doth many motherly offices in preparing it: so is not
friendship then onely to be esteemed, when she is delivered
of a Letter, or any other reall office, but in her continuall
propensnesse and inclination to do it. This hath made me
easie in pardoning my long silences, and in promising my
self your forgivenesse for not answering your Letter sooner.
For my purpose of proceeding in the profession of the law,
so farre as to a title you may be pleased to correct that
imagination, wheresoever you finde it. I ever thought the
study of it my best entertainment, and pastime, but I
have no ambition, nor designe upon the style. Of my
Anniversaries, the fault that I acknowledge in my selfe, is
to have descended to print any thing in verse, which though
it have excuse even in our times, by men who professe, and
practise much gravitie; yet I confesse I wonder how I
declined to it, and do not pardon my self: But for the other
part of the imputation of having said too much, my defence

is, that my purpose was to say as well as I could: for since I never saw the Gentlewoman, I cannot be understood to have bound my self to have spoken just truths, but I would not be thought to have gone about to praise her, or any other in rime; except I took such a person, as might be capable of all that I could say. If any of those Ladies think that Mistris *Drewry* was not so, let that Lady make her self fit for all those praises in the book, and they shall be hers. Sir, this messenger makes so much haste that I cry
10 you mercy for spending any time of this letter in other imployment than thanking you for yours. I hope before *Christmas* to see *England*, and kisse your hand, which shall ever, (if it disdain not that office) hold all the keyes of the libertie and affection, and all the faculties of

Your most affectionate servant,

J. D.

Paris the 14th of
Aprill, here, 1612.

3. To *Sir Henry Goodyere*

[about publishing his poems]

ONE thing more I must tell you; but so softly, that I am
20 loath to hear my self: and so softly, that if that good Lady were in the room, with you and this Letter, she might not hear. It is, that I am brought to a necessity of printing my Poems, and addressing them to my L. Chamberlain. This I mean to do forthwith; not for much publique view, but at mine own cost, a few Copies. I apprehend some incongruities in the resolution; and I know what I shall suffer from many interpretations: but I am at an end, of much considering that; and, if I were as startling in that kinde, as ever I was, yet in this particular, I am under an unescap-
30 able necessity, as I shall let you perceive, when I see you.

By this occasion I am made a Rhapsoder of mine own rags,
and that cost me more diligence, to seek them, then it did
to make them. This made me aske to borrow that old book
of you, which it will be too late to see, for that use, when I
see you: for I must do this, as a valediction to the world,
before I take Orders. But this is it, I am to aske you;
whether you ever made any such use of the letter in verse,
A nostre Countesse chez vous, as that I may not put it
in, amongst the rest to persons of that rank; for I desire
very very much, that something should bear her name in
the book, and I would be just to my written words to my
L. Harrington, to write nothing after that. I pray tell me as
soon as you can, if I be at liberty to insert that; for if you
have by any occasion applied any pieces of it, I see not, that
it will be discerned, when it appears in the whole piece.

   Vigilia St. Tho.

      1614

SERMONS

1. *Late Repentance*

(Donne's earliest extant Sermon)

AND so also, if we have seen a man prodigal of his own soul,
and run on in a course of sin, all his life, except there appear
very evident sign of resumption into God's grace, at his end,
Exhaeredatus Creditur, we have just cause to be afraid, that
he is disinherited. If any such sinner seem to thee to repent at his end, *Fateor vobis non negamus, quod petit*, saith
St. Augustin: I confess, we ought not to deny him, any
help that he desires in that late extremity: *Sed non praesumi-
mus quia bene exit*, I dare not assure you, that that man dyes
in a good state; he adds that vehemence, *non praesumo, non
vos fallo, non praesumo*: I should but deceive you, if I should
assure you, that such a man dyed well. There was one good

and happy Thief, that stole a Salvation, at the crucifying of
Christ; but in him, that was throughly true, which is
proverbially spoken, *Occasio facit furem*, the opportunity
made him a thief: and when there is such another opportunity
there may be such another theif; when Christ is to dye again,
we may presume of mercy, upon such a late repentance at
our death. The preventing Grace of God, made him lay
violent hands upon heaven. But when thou art a Prodigal
of thy soul, will God be a prodigal too, for thy sake, and
10 betray and prostitute the kingdome of Heaven for a sigh,
or a groan, in which thy pain may have a greater part than
thy repentance? God can raise up children out of the stones
of the street, and therefore he might be as liberal as he
would of his people, and suffer them to be sold for old shoes;
but Christ will not sell his birth-right for a messe of pottage,
the kingdome of Heaven for the dole at a Funeral. Heaven
is not to be had in exchange for an Hospital, or a Chantry,
or a Colledge erected in thy last will: It is not onely the sell-
ing all we have that must buy that pearl, which represents
20 the Kingdome of Heaven; The giving of all that we have
to the poor, at our death, will not do it; the pearl must be
sought, and found before, in an even and constant course
of Sanctification; we must be thrifty all our life, or we shall
be to⟨o⟩ poor for that purchase.

2. *Queen Elizabeth and King James*

As the Rule is true, *Cum de Malo principe posteri tacent,
manifestum est vilem facere praesentem*, when men dare not
speak of the vices of a Prince that is dead, it is certain that
the Prince that is alive proceeds in the same vices; so the
inversion of the Rule is true too, *Cum de bono principe
30 loquuntur*, when men may speak freely of the virtues of a
dead Prince, it is an evident argument, that the present

Prince practises the same virtues; for if he did not, he would
not love to hear of them. Of *her*, we may say (that which
was well said, and therefore it were pity it should not be
once truly said, for so it was not, when it was first said to
the Emperor *Julian*) *nihil humile, aut abjectum cogitavit,
quia novit de se semper loquendum*; she knew the world would
talk of her after her death, and therefore she did such things
all her life were worthy to be talked of. Of her glorious suc-
cessor, and our gracious Soveraign, we may say; *Onerosum
est succedere bono Principi*, It would have troubled any
king but *him*, to have come in succession, and in comparison
with such a *Queen*. And in them both we may observe the
unsearchableness of the ways of God; of them both, we
may say, *Dominus fecit, It is the Lord that hath done it, and
it is wonderful in our eyes*: First, That a *woman* and a *maid*
should have all the wars of Christendom in her contemplation, and govern and ballance them all; And then, That a
King, born and bred in a *warlike Nation*, and so accustomed
to the *sword*, as that it had been directed upon his own
person, in the *strength* of his age, and in his *Infancy*, in his
Cradle, in his *mothers belly*, should yet have the *blessed spirit
of peace* so abundantly in him, as that by his Councils, and
his authority, he should sheath all the swords of Christendom
again. *De forti egressa dulcedo*, sweetness is come out of the
strong, in a stranger manner, then when Sampson said so in
his riddle; And howsoever another wise King found it true,
*Anima saturata calcabit favum, The person that is full despiseth
honey*, they that are glutted with the benefits of peace,
would fain change for a war; yet the wisest King of all hath
pronounced for our King, *Beati, pacifici, Blessed are the
peace-makers*. If subjects will not apprehend it with joy
here, the King himself shall joy hereafter, for, Therefore
(says that Gospel) Therefore, because he was a peace-maker,
he shall be called *The Childe of God*. Though then these two

great Princes (of whom the one *con-regnat Christo*, reigns now with Christ, the other reigns over us *vice Christi*, for Christ,) were near in blood, yet thus were they nearest of kin, *quod uterque optimus*, That they were both better then any other, and equal to one another. *Dignus alter eligi, alter eligere*, That she was fittest in that fullness of years, to be chosen and assum'd into heaven, and he fittest (as Saint *Paul* did it because it was behoofeful for his brethren) to choose to stay upon earth, for our protection, and for our
10 direction; because (as in all Princes it is) *vita principis perpetua censura*, There cannot be a more powerful increpation upon the subjects excesses, then when they see the King deny himself those pleasures which they take.

As then this place where we all stand now, was the *Sanctuary* whither we all resorted this day, to receive the assurance of our safety, in the proclamation of his undoubted title to this Kingdom, so let it be *our Altar* now, where we may sacrifice our humble thanks to God, first, that he always gave the King a just, and a religious patience of not attempt-
20 ing a coming into this Kingdom, till God emptied the throne here, by translating that Queen to a throne more glorious. Perchance he was not without tentations from other men to have done otherwise. But, *Ad Principatum per obsequium venit*, he came to be King by his obedience, his obedience to the law of *Nature*, and the laws of this *Kingdom*, to which some other King would have disputed, whether he should have obey'd or no. *Cum omnia faceret imperare ut deberet, nihil fecit, ut imperaret*; All his Actions, all that he did, show him fit for this Crown, and yet he would do nothing to
30 anticipate that Crown.

Next let us pour out our thanks to God, that in his entrance he was beholden to no *by-religion*. The *Papists* could not make him place any hopes upon them, nor the *Puritans* make him entertain any fears from them; but his God and

our God, as he brought him *via lactea*, by the sweet way of
Peace, that flows with milk and hony, so he brought him *via
Regia*, by the direct and plain way, without any deviation or
descent into ignoble flatteries, or servile humoring of any
persons or factions. Which noble, and Christian courage he
expressed more manifestly, when, after that infamous *powder
treason*, the intended dissolution, and conflagration of this
state (that plot that even amaz'd and astonished *the Devil*,
and seem'd a miracle even in hell, that treason, which,
whosoever wishes might be covered now, is sorry that it 10
was discovered then, whosoever wishes that it might be
forgotten, wishes that it had proceeded. And therefore let
our tongue cleave unto the roof of our mouths, if we do not
confess his loving kindness before the Lord, and his wonderful works before the Sons of men) Then I say, did his Majesty
show this Christian courage of his more manifestly, when he
sent the profession of his Religion, *The Apology of the Oath
of Allegeance*, and his opinion of the *Romane Antichrist*, in
all languages, to all Princes of Christendom. By occasion
of which Book, though there have risen twenty *Rabshakes*, 20
who have rail'd against our God in railing against our
Religion, and twenty *Shemeis*, who have railed against the
person of his sacred Majesty (for, I may pronounce that the
number of them who have bark'd, and snarl'd at that book
in writing, is scarce less than fourty) yet scarce one of them
all hath undertaken the arguments of that book, but either
repeated, and perchance enlarged those things which their
own Authours had shovel'd together of that subject (that is,
The Popes Temporal power) or else they have bent themselves
maliciously, insolently, sacrilegiously, against the person of 30
his Majesty; and the *Pope* may be *Antichrist* still, for any
thing they have said to the contrary. It belonged only to
him, whom no earthly King may enter into comparison with,
the King of Heaven, *Christ Jesus*, to say, *Those that thou*

gavest to me have I kept, and none of them is lost. And even
in him, in *Christ Jesus* himself, that admitted one exception,
Judas the childe of perdition was lost. Our King cannot say
that *none* of his subjects are fled to Rome; but his vigilancy
at home hath wrought so, as that *fewer* are gone from our
Universities thither, in his, then in former times; and his
Books abroad have wrought so, that much greater, and considerable persons are come to us then are gone from us. I
add that particular (from our *Universities*) because we see,
10 that since those men whom our Universities had bred, and
graduated before they went thither, (of which the number
was great, for many years of the Queens time) are worne
out amongst them, and dead; those whom they make up
there, whom they have had from their first youth there, who
have received all their Learning from their beggarly and
fragmentary way of Dictates there, and were never grounded
in our Schools nor Universities, have prov'd but weak main-
tainers of that cause, compar'd with those men of the first
times.

3. *Death a Rapture and Ecstasy*

20 *DEATH and life are in the power of the tongue,* sayes *Solomon,*[1]
in another sense; and in this sense too, If my tongue,
suggested by my heart, and by my heart rooted in faith,
can say, *Non moriar, non moriar*; If I can say, (and my conscience doe not tell me, that I belye mine owne state) if I
can say, That the blood of my Saviour runs in my veines,
That the breath of his Spirit quickens all my purposes, that
all my deaths have their Resurrection, all my sins their
remorses, all my rebellions their reconciliations, I will
harken no more after this question, as it is intended *de morte*

[1] Prov. 18. 21

naturali, of a naturall death, I know I must die that death, what care I? nor *de morte spirituali*, the death of sin, I know I doe, and shall die so; why despaire I?[1] but I will finde out another death, *mortem raptus*, a death of rapture, and of extasie, that death which S. *Paul* died more then once,[2] The death which S. *Gregory* speaks of, *Divina contemplatio quoddam sepulchrum animæ*,[3] The contemplation of God, and heaven, is a kinde of buriall, and Sepulchre, and rest of the soule; and in this death of rapture, and extasie, in this death of the Contemplation of my interest in my Saviour, I shall finde my self, and all my sins enterred, and entombed in his wounds, and like a Lily in Paradise, out of red earth, I shall see my soule rise out of his blade, in a candor, and in an innocence, contracted there, acceptable in the sight of his Father.

Though I have been dead, in the delight of sin, so that that of S. *Paul*, *That a Widow that liveth in pleasure, is dead while she liveth*,[4] be true of my soule, that so, *viduatur, gratiâ mortuâ*, when Christ is dead, not for the soule, but in the soule, that the soule hath no sense of Christ, *Viduatur anima*, the soul is a Widow, and no Dowager, she hath lost her husband, and hath nothing from him; yea[5] though *I have made a Covenant with death, and have been at an agreement with hell*, and in a vain confidence have said to my self, *that when the over-flowing scourge shall passe through, it shall not come to me*, yet God shall annull that covenant, he shall bring that scourge, that is, some medicinall correction upon me, and so give me a participation of all the stripes of his son; he shall give me a sweat, that is, some horrour, and religious feare, and so give me a participation of his Agony; he shall give me a diet, perchance want, and penury, and so a participation of his fasting; and if he draw blood, if he kill me, all this shall be but *Mors raptus*, a death of rapture towards

[1] 2 Cor. 12.   [2] Acts. 9.   [3] Greg.   [4] 1 Tim. 5. 6.   [5] Esay 28. 15.

2179.36   K

him, into a heavenly, and assured Contemplation, that I
have a part in all his passion, yea such an intire interest in
his whole passion, as though all that he did, or suffered, had
been done, and suffered for my soule alone; *Quasi moriens,*
& ecce vivo:[1] some shew of death I shall have, for I shall sin;
and some shew of death again, for I shall have a dissolution
of this Tabernacle; *Sed ecce vivo,* still the Lord of life will keep
me alive, and that with an *Ecce,* Behold, I live; that is, he
will declare, and manifest my blessed state to me; I shall not
10 sit in the shadow of death; no nor I shall not sit in darknesse;
his gracious purpose shall evermore be upon me, and I shall
ever discerne that gracious purpose of his; I shall not die,
nor I shall not doubt that I shall; If I be dead within doores,
(If I have sinned in my heart) why, *Suscitavit in domo,*[2]
Christ gave a Resurrection to the Rulers daughter within
doores, in the house; If I be dead in the gate, (If I have
sinned in the gates of my soule) in mine Eies, or Eares, or
Hands, in actuall sins, why, *suscitavit in porta,*[3] Christ gave
a Resurrection to the young man at the gate of *Naim.* If
20 I be dead in the grave, (in customary, and habituall sins)
why, *Suscitavit in Sepulchro,* Christ gave a Resurrection to
Lazarus in the grave too.[4] If God give me *mortem raptus,* a
death of rapture, of extasie, of fervent Contemplation of
Christ Jesus, a Transfusion, a Transplantation, a Trans-
migration, a Transmutation into him, (for good digestion
brings alwaies assimilation, certainly, if I come to a true
meditation upon Christ, I come to a conformity with Christ)
this is principally that *Pretiosa mors Sanctorum, Pretious in the*
sight of the Lord, is the death of his Saints,[5] by which they are
30 dead and buryed, and risen again in Christ Jesus: pretious
is that death, by which we apply that pretious blood to
our selves, and grow strong enough by it, to meet *Davids*

---

[1] 2 Cor. 6. 9. [2] Mat. 9. 23. [3] Luke 7. 11. [4] John 11.
[5] Psal. 116. 15.

question, *Quis homo?* what man? with Christs answer, *Ego homo*, I am the man, in whom whosoever abideth, shall not see death.

4. *Prayer*

BUT when we meet in Gods house, though, by occasion, there be no Sermon, yet if we meet to pray, we pay our debt, we doe our duty; so doe we not, if we meet at a Sermon, without prayer. The Church is the house of prayer, so, as that upon occasion, preaching may be left out, but never a house of preaching, so, as that Prayer may be left out. And for the debt of prayer, God will not be paid, with money of our 10 owne coyning, (with sudden, extemporall, inconsiderate prayer) but with currant money, that beares the Kings Image, and inscription; The Church of God, by his Ordinance, hath set his stampe, upon a Liturgie and Service, for his house. *Audit Deus in corde cogitantis, quod nec ipse audit, qui cogitat*, sayes S. Bernard: God hears the very first motions of a man's heart, which, that man, till he proceed to a farther consideration, doth not heare, not feele, not deprehend in himselfe.

That soule, that is accustomed to direct her selfe to God, 20 upon every occasion, that, as a flowre at Sun-rising, conceives a sense of God, in every beame of his, and spreads and dilates it selfe towards him, in a thankfulnesse, in every small blessing that he sheds upon her; that soule, that as a flowre at the Suns declining, contracts and gathers in, and shuts up her selfe, as though she had received a blow, when soever she heares her Saviour wounded by a⟨n⟩ oath, or blasphemy, or execration; that soule, who, whatsoever string be strucken in her, base or treble, her high or her low estate, is ever tun'd toward God, that soule 30 prayes sometimes when it does not know that it prayes.

I heare that man name God, and aske him what said you,
and perchance he cannot tell; but I remember, that he
casts forth some of those *ejaculationes animæ,* (as S. *August:*
calls them) some of those darts of a devout soule, which,
though they have not particular deliberations, and be not
formall prayers, yet they are the *indicia,* pregnant evi-
dences and blessed fruits of a religious custome; much
more it is true, which S. *Bernard* saies there, of them, *Deus
audit,* God heares that voice of the heart, which the heart
10 it selfe heares not, that is, at first considers not. Those
occasionall and transitory prayers, and those fixed and
stationary prayers, for which, many times, we binde our
selves to private prayer at such a time, are payments of this
debt, in such peeces, and in such summes, as God, no doubt,
accepts at our hands. But yet the solemne dayes of payment, are the Sabbaths of the Lord, and the place of this
payment, is the house of the Lord, where, as *Tertullian*
expresses it, *Agmine facto,* we muster our forces together,
and besiege God; that is, not taking up every tatter'd fellow,
20 every sudden ragge or fragment of speech, that rises from
our tongue, or our affections, but mustering up those words,
which the Church hath levied for that service, in the Con-
fessions, and Absolutions, and Collects, and Litanies of the
Church. we pay this debt, and we receive our acquittance.

* * *

Begin therefore to pay these debts to thy selfe betimes;
for, as we told you at beginning, some you are to tender at
noone, some at evening. Even at your noon and warmest
Sun-shine of prosperity, you owe your selves a true information, how you came by that prosperity, who gave it you,
30 and why he gave it. Let not the Olive boast of her own
fatnesse, nor the Fig-tree of her own sweetnesse, nor the
Vine of her own fruitfulnesse, for we were all but Brambles.

Let no man say, I could not misse a fortune, for I have
studied all my youth; How many men have studied more
nights, then he hath done hours, and studied themselves
blinde, and mad in the Mathematiques, and yet withers in
beggery in a corner? Let him never adde, But I studied in
a usefull and gainfull profession; How many have done so
too, and yet never compassed the favour of a Judge? And
how many that have had all that, have struck upon a Rock,
even at full Sea, and perished there? In their Grandfathers
& great Grandfathers, in a few generations, whosoever is
greatest now, must say, With this Staffe came I over Jordan;
nay, without any staffe came I over Jordan, for he had in
them at first, a beginning of nothing. As for spiritual happinesse, *Non volentis, nec currentis, sed miserentis Dei,* It is not
in him that would run, nor in him that doth, but only in God
that prospers his course; so for the things of this world, it
is in vain to rise early, and to lie down late, and to eat the
bread of sorrow, for, *nisi Dominus ædificaverit, nisi Dominus
custodierit,* except the Lord build the house, they labour in
vaine; except the Lord keep the City, the watchman waketh
but in vain. Come not therefore to say, I studied more
than my fellows, and therefore am richer than my fellows,
but say, God that gave me my contemplations at first, gave
me my practice after, and hath given me his blessing now.
How many men have worn their braines upon other studies,
and spent their time and themselves therein? how many
men have studied more in thine own profession, and yet, for
diffidence in themselves, or some disfavour from others,
have not had thy practice? How many men have been
equall to thee, in study, in practice, and in getting too, and
yet upon a wanton confidence, that that world would
alwayes last, or upon the burden of many children, and an
expensive breeding of them, or for other reasons, which God
hath found in his wayes, are left upon the sand at last, in

a low fortune? whilest the Sun shines upon thee in all these, pay thy self the debt, of knowing whence, and why all this came, for else thou canst not know how much, or how little is thine, nor thou canst not come to restore that which is none of thine, but unjustly wrung from others. Pay therefore this debt of surveying thine estate, and then pay thy selfe thine own too, by a chearfull enjoying and using that which is truly thine, and doe not deny nor defraud thy selfe of those things which are thine, and so become a wretched debtor, to thy back, or to thy belly, as though the world had not enough, or God knew not what were enough for thee.

Pay this debt to thy selfe of looking into thy debts, of surveying, of severing, of serving thy selfe with that which is truly thine, at thy noone, in the best of thy fortune, and in the strength of thine understanding; that when thou commest to pay thy other, thy last debt to thy self, which is, to open a doore out of this world, by the dissolution of body and soule, thou have not all thy money to tell over when the Sun is ready to set, all the account to make of every bag of money, and of every quillet of land, whose it is, and whether it be his that looks for it from thee, or his from whom it was taken by thee; whether it belong to thine heire, that weepes joyfull tears behinde the curtain, or belong to him that weeps true, and bloody teares, in the hole in a prison. There will come a time, when that land that thou leavest shall not be his land, when it shall be no bodies land, when it shall be no land, for the earth must perish; there will be a time when there shall be no Mannors, no Acres in the world, and yet there shall lie Mannors and Acres upon thy soul, when land shall be no more, when time shall be no more, and thou passe away, not into the land of the living, but of eternall death. Then the Accuser will be ready to interline the schedules of thy debts, thy sins, and insert false debts, by abusing an over-tendernesse, which may

be in thy conscience then, in thy last sicknesse, in thy death-
bed: Then he will be ready to adde a cyphar more to thy
debts, and make hundreds thousands, and abuse the faint-
nesse which may be in thy conscience then, in thy last sicknesse, in thy death-bed. Then he will be ready to abuse
even thy confidence in God, and bring thee to think, that
as a Pirate ventures boldly home, though all that he hath be
stoln, if he be rich enough to bribe for a pardon; so, howsoever those families perish whom thou hast ruined, and
those whole parishes whom thou hast depopulated, thy soule 10
may goe confidently home too, if thou bribe God then, with
an Hospitall or a Fellowship in a Colledge, or a Legacy to
any pious use in apparance, and in the eye of the world.

5. *Mercy and Judgment*

WE begin with that which is elder than our beginning, and
shall over-live our end, The mercy of God. *I will sing of thy
mercy and judgement*, sayes *David*; when we fixe our selves
upon the meditation and modulation of the mercy of God,
even his judgements cannot put us out of tune, but we shall
sing, and be chearefull, even in them. As God made grasse
for beasts, before he made beasts, and beasts for man, before 20
he made man: As in that first generation, the Creation, so in
the regeneration, our re-creating, he begins with that which
was necessary for that which followes, Mercy before Judgement. Nay, to say that Mercy was first, is but to post-date
mercy; to preferre mercy but so, is to diminish mercy; The
names of first or last derogate from it, for first and last are
but ragges of time, and his mercy hath no relation to time,
no limitation in time, it is not first, nor last, but eternall,
everlasting. Let the Devill make me so far desperate as to
conceive a time when there was no mercy, and he hath made 30

me so far an atheist, as to conceive a time when there was
no God; if I despoile him of his mercy, any one minute, and
say, now God hath no mercy, for that minute I discontinue
his very Godhead, and his beeing. Later Grammarians have
wrung the name of mercy out of misery: *Misericordia prae-
sumit miseriam*, say these, there could be no subsequent
mercy, if there were no precedent misery; But the true roote
of the word mercy, through all the Prophets, is *Racham*,
and *Racham* is *diligere*, to love; as long as there hath been
10 love (and *God is love*) there hath been mercy: And mercy
considered externally, and in the practise and in the effect,
began not at the helping of man, when man was fallen and
become miserable, but at the making of man, when man
was nothing. So then, here we consider not mercy as it is
radically in God, and an essentiall attribute of his, but
productively in us, as it is an action, a working upon us,
and that more especially, as God takes all occasions to
exercise that action, and to shed that mercy upon us: for
particular mercies are feathers of his wings, and that prayer,
20 *Lord let thy mercy lighten upon us, as our trust is in thee*, is
our birdlime; particular mercies are that cloud of Quailes
which hovered over the host of Israel, and that prayer,
Lord let thy mercy lighten upon us, is our net to catch, our
Gomer to fill of those Quailes. The aire is not so full of Moats,
of Atomes, as the Church is of Mercies; and as we can suck
in no part of aire, but we take in those Moats, those Atomes;
so here in the Congregation we cannot suck in a word from
the preacher, we cannot speak, we cannot sigh a prayer to
God, but that that whole breath and aire is made of mercy.
30 But we call not upon you from this Text, to consider Gods
ordinary mercy, that which he exhibites to all in the ministery
of his Church; nor his miraculous mercy, his extraordinary
deliverances of States and Churches; but we call upon
particular Consciences, by occasion of this Text, to call to

minde Gods occasionall mercies to them; such mercies as
a regenerate man will call mercies, though a naturall man
would call them accidents, or occurrences, or contingencies;
A man wakes at midnight full of unclean thoughts, and he
heares a passing Bell; this is an occasionall mercy, if he call
that his own knell, and consider how unfit he was to be
called out of the world then, how unready to receive that
voice, *Foole, this night they shall fetch away thy soule*. The
adulterer, whose eye waites for the twy-light, goes forth,
and casts his eyes upon forbidden houses, and would enter, 10
and sees a *Lord have mercy upon us* upon the doore; this is
an occasionall mercy, if this bring him to know that they
who lie sick of the plague within, passe through a furnace,
but by Gods grace, to heaven; and hee without, carries his
own furnace to hell, his lustfull loines to everlasting perdition. What an occasionall mercy had *Balaam*, when his
Asse Catechized him: What an occasionall mercy had one
Theefe, when the other catechized him so, *Art not thou
afraid being under the same condemnation?* What an occasionall mercy had all they that saw that, when the Devil 20
himself fought for the name of Jesus, and wounded the
sons of *Sceva* for exorcising in the name of Jesus, with
that indignation, with that increpation, *Jesus we know, and
Paul we know, but who are ye?* If I should declare what God
hath done (done occasionally) for my soule, where he in-
structed me for feare of falling, where he raised me when
I was fallen, perchance you would rather fixe your thoughts
upon my illnesse, and wonder at that, than at Gods goodnesse, and glorifie him in that; rather wonder at my sins,
then at his mercies, rather consider how ill a man I was, 30
than how good a God he is. If I should inquire upon what
occasion God elected me, and writ my name in the book of
Life, I should sooner be afraid that it were not so, then
finde a reason why it should be so. God made Sun and

Moon to distinguish seasons, and day, and night, and we
cannot have the fruits of the earth but in their seasons:
But God hath made no decree to distinguish the seasons
of his mercies; In paradise, the fruits were ripe, the first
minute, and in heaven it is alwaies Autumne, his mercies
are ever in their maturity. We ask *panem quotidianum*, our
daily bread, and God never sayes you should have come
yesterday, he never sayes you must againe to morrow, but
to day if you will heare his voice, to day he will heare you. If
10 some King of the earth have so large an extent of Dominion,
in North, and South, as that he hath Winter and Summer
together in his Dominions, so large an extent East and West,
as that he hath day and night together in his Dominions,
much more hath God mercy and judgement together: He
brought light out of darknesse, not out of a lesser light; he
can bring thy Summer out of Winter, though thou have no
Spring; though in the wayes of fortune, or understanding,
or conscience, thou have been benighted till now, wintred
and frozen, clouded and eclypsed, damped and benummed,
20 smothered and stupified till now, now God comes to thee,
not as in the dawning of the day, not as in the bud of the
spring, but as the Sun at noon to illustrate all shadowes,
as the sheaves in harvest, to fill all penuries, all occasions
invite his mercies, and all times are his seasons.

6. *A Better Resurrection*

Now what was this that they qualified and dignified by
that addition, *The better Resurrection?* Is it called better,
in that it is better then this life, and determined in that
comparison, and degree of betternesse, and no more? Is
it better than those honours, and preferments which that
30 King offered them, and determined in that comparison,

and no more? Or better then other men shall have at the
last day, (for all men shall have a Resurrection) and determined in that? Or, as S. *Chrysostome* takes it, is it but a
better Resurrection then that in the former part of this
Text, where dead children are restored to their mothers
alive again? Is it but a better Resurrection in some of
these senses? Surely better in a higher sense than any of
these; It is a supereminent degree of glory, a larger measure
of glory, then every man, who in a generall happinesse, is
made partaker of the Resurrection of the righteous, is made 10
partaker of.

Beloved, There is nothing so little in heaven, as that we
can expresse it; But if wee could tell you the fulnesse of a
soul there, what that fulnesse is; the infinitenesse of that
glory there, how far that infinitenesse goes; the Eternity
of that happinesse there, how long that happinesse lasts;
if we could make you know all this, yet this *Better Resurrec-*
tion is a heaping, even of that Fulnesse, and an enlarging,
even of that Infinitenesse, and an extention, even of that
eternity of happinesse; For, all these, this Fulnesse, this 20
Infinitenesse, this Eternity are in all the Resurrections of
the Righteous, and this is a *better Resurrection;* We may
almost say, it is something more then Heaven; for, all that
have any Resurrection to life, have all heaven; And something more than God; for, all that have any Resurrection
to life, have all God; and yet these shall have a better
Resurrection. Amorous soule, ambitious soule, covetous
soule, voluptuous soule, what wouldest thou have in heaven?
What doth thy holy amorousnesse, thy holy covetousnesse,
thy holy ambition, and voluptuousnesse most carry thy 30
desire upon? Call it what thou wilt; think it what thou
canst; think it something that thou canst not think; and
all this thou shalt have, if thou have any Resurrection
unto life; and yet there is a *Better Resurrection.* When I

consider what I was in my parents loynes (a substance
unworthy of a word, unworthy of a thought) when I consider what I am now, (a Volume of diseases bound up together, a dry cynder, if I look for naturall, for radicall
moisture, and yet a Spunge, a bottle of overflowing Rheumes,
if I consider accidentall; an aged childe, a gray-headed
Infant, and but the ghost of mine own youth) When I
consider what I shall be at last, by the hand of death, in
my grave, (first, but Putrifaction, and then, not so much
10 as Putrifaction, I shall not be able to send forth so much
as an ill ayre, not any ayre at all, but shall be all insipid,
tastlesse, savourlesse dust; for a while, all wormes, and
after a while, not so much as wormes, sordid, senslesse,
namelesse dust) When I consider the past, and present,
and future state of this body, in this world, I am able to
conceive, able to expresse the worst that can befall it in
nature, and the worst that can be inflicted upon it by man,
or fortune; But the least degree of glory that God hath
prepared for that body in heaven, I am not able to expresse,
20 not able to conceive.

That man comes with a Barly corn in his hand, to measure
the compasse of the Firmament (and when will he have done
that work, by that way?) he comes with a grain of dust in
his scales, to weigh the whole body of the world, (and when
will he have done that work, that way?) that bids his heart
imagine, or his language declare, or his wit compare the
least degree of the glory of any good mans Resurrection;
And yet, there is a *Better Resurrection*. A *Better Resurrection*
reserved for them, and appropriated to them *That fulfill the*
30 *sufferings of Christ, in their flesh,* by Martyrdome, and so
become witnesses to that Conveyance which he hath sealed
with his blood, by shedding their blood; and glorifie him
upon earth (as far as it is possible for man) by the same way
that he hath glorified them in heaven; and are admitted

to such a conformity with Christ, as that (if we may have
leave to expresse it so) they have died for one another.

Neither is this Martyrdome, and so this *Better Resurrection*,
appropriated to a reall, and actuall, and absolute dying for
Christ; but every suffering of ours, by which suffering, he
may be glorified, is a degree of Martyrdome, and so a degree
of improving, and bettering our Resurrection. For as S.
Ierome sayes, *That chastity is a perpetuall Martyrdome*, So
every war maintained by us, against our own desires, is a
Martyrdome too. In a word, to do good for Gods glory, 10
brings us to a Good, but to suffer for his glory, brings us to
a *Better Resurrection*; And, to suffer patiently, brings us
to a Good, but to suffer chearefully, and more then that,
thankfully, brings us to a *Better Resurrection*. If all the
torments of all the afflicted men, from *Abel*, to that soul
that groanes in the Inquisition, or that gaspes upon his
death-bed, at this minute, were upon one man at once, all
that had no proportion to the least torment of hell; nay if
all the torments which all the damned in hell have suffered,
from *Cain* to this minute, were at once upon one soul, so, 20
as that soul for all that, might know that those torments
should have an end, though after a thousand millions of
millions of Generations, all that would have no proportion
to any of the torments of hell; because, the extention of
those torments, and their everlastingnesse, hath more of
the nature of torment, and of the nature of hell in it, then
the intensnesse, and the vehemency thereof can have. So,
if all the joyes, of all the men that have had all their hearts
desires, were con-centred in one heart, all that would not
be as a spark in his Chimney, to the generall conflagration 30
of the whole world, in respect of the least joy, that that
soule is made partaker of, that departs from this world,
immediately after a pardon received, and reconciliation
sealed to him, for all his sins; No doubt but he shall have

a good Resurrection; But then, we cannot doubt neither, but that to him that hath been carefull in all his wayes, and yet crost in all his wayes, to him whose daily bread hath been affliction, and yet is satisfied as with marrow, and with fatnesse, with that bread of affliction, and not only contented in, but glad of that affliction, no doubt but to him is reserved a *Better Resurrection*; Every Resurrection is more than we can think, but this is more then that more. Almighty God inform us, and reveale unto us, what this
10 *Better Resurrection* is, by possessing us of it; And make the hastening to it, one degree of addition in it. Come Lord Jesus, come quickly to the consummation of that Kingdome which thou hast purchased for us, with the inestimable price of thine incorruptible blood. *Amen.*

7. *Religious Assurance*

O MY lord, *send I pray thee, by the hand of him whom thou wilt send* . . . These words then (though some have made that interpretation of them, and truly, not without a faire apparance, and probability, and verisimilitude) doe not necessarily imply a slacknesse in *Moses* zeale, that he desired
20 not affectionately, and earnestly the deliverance of his Nation from the pressures of Aegypt; nor doe they imply any diffidence, or distrust, that God could not, or would not endow him with faculties fit for that imployment; But as a thoughtfull man, a pensive, a considerative man, that stands still for a while, with his eyes fixed upon the ground, before his feete, when he casts up his head, hath presently, instantly the Sun, or the heavens for his object, he sees not a tree, nor a house, nor a steeple by the way, but as soon as his eye is departed from the earth where it was long fixed,
30 the next thing he sees is the Sun or the heavens; so when

Moses had fixed himselfe long upon the consideration of his own insufficiency for this service, when he tooke his eye from that low peece of ground, Himselfe, considered as he was then, he fell upon no tree, no house, no steeple, no such consideration as this, God may endow me, improve me, exalt me, qualifie me with faculties fit for this service, but his first object was that which presented an infallibility with it, Christ Jesus himselfe, the Messias himselfe.

8. *Sin and Death*

THE Graces, and blessings of God, that is, means of salvation, are so aboundantly poured upon the Christian Church, as that the triumphant Church if they needed means, might fear they should want them. And of these means and blessings, *long life*, as it is a *Modell* and abridgement of *Eternity*, and a *help* to *Eternitie*, is one; and one in this Text, *The childe shall die* 100. *yeares old*. But shall we receive good from God, and not receive evill too? shall I shed upon you *Lumen visionis*, the light of that vision, which God hath afforded me in this Prophecie, the light of his countenance, and his gracious blessings upon you, and not lay upon you *Onus visionis*, as the Prophets speak often, The burthen of that vision which I have seen in this Text too? It was a scorn to *David*, that his servants were half cloath'd; The *Samaritane* woman beleeved, that if she might see Christ, he would tell her all things: Christ promises of the *Holy Ghost*, that he should lead them into *all Truth*: And the Apostles discharge in his office was, that he had spoken to them *all Truth*: And therefore lest I should be defective in that integritie, I say with Saint *Augustine, Non vos fallo, non praesumo, non vos fallo*; I will not be so bold with you as flatter you, I will not presume so much on your weak-nesse, as to go about to deceive you, as though there were

nothing but blessing in God, but show you the Commina-
tion, and judgement of this Text too, that though *the childe
should die a hundred years old, yet the sinner being a hundred
years old shall be accursed.* If God had not lengthened his
childes life, extended my dayes, but taken me in the sinnes
of my youth, where had I been, may every soul here say?
And where would you be too, if no man should tell you,
that though *The childe should die a hundred years old, yet
the sinner being a hundred years old shall be accursed?* What
10 can be certain in this world, if even the mercy of God admit
a variation? what can be endlesse here, if even the mercy
of God receive a determination? and *sin* doth vary the
nature, *sin* doth determine even the infinitenesse of the
mercy of God himself, for though *The childe shall die a
hundred yeares old*, yet *the sinner being a hundred years old
shall be accursed.* Disconsolate soul, dejected spirit, bruised
and broken, ground and trodden, attenuated, evaporated,
annihilated heart come back; heare thy *reprieve,* and sue
for thy *pardon;* God will not take thee away in thy sins,
20 thou shalt have time to repent, *The childe shall die a hundred
years old.* But then lame and decrepit soul, gray and in-
veterate sinner, behold the full ears of corn blasted with a
mildew, behold this long day shutting up in such a night,
as shall never see light more, the night of death; in which,
the deadliest pang of thy *Death* will be thine *Immortality:* In
this especially shalt thou die, that thou canst not die, when
thou art dead; but must live dead for ever: for *The sinner
being a hundred yeers old, shall be accursed,* he shall be so
for ever.

9. *From Donne's Last Sermon*

30 THE ancient *Romans* had a certain tendernesse and detesta-
tion of the name of death, they could not name death, no,
not in their wills. There they could not say *Si mori contigerit,*

but *si quid humanitus contingat*, nor if, or when I dye, but
when the course of nature is accomplished upon me. To us
that speake dayly of the *death* of *Christ*, (he was *crucified,
dead* and *buried*) can the memory or the mention of our owne
death bee yrkesome or bitter? There are in these latter times
amongst us, that name death frely enogh, and the death
of *God*, but in *blasphemous oathes* and *execrations*. Miserable
men, who shall therefore bee said never to have named
Jesus, because they have named him *too often*. And therefore
heare *Jesus* say, *Nescivi vos*, I *never knew you*, because they 10
made themselves *too familiar* with him. *Moses* and *Elias*
talkt with *Christ* of his *death*, only, in *a holy* and *joyfull
sense* of the *benefit* which *they* and *all* the world were to
receive by that. *Discourses* of *Religion* should not be *out*
of *curiosity*, but to *edification*. And then they talkt with
Christ of his *death* at that time, when he was in the greatest
height of glory that ever he admitted in this world, that is,
his *transfiguration*. And wee are afraid to speake to the *great
men* of this world of their *death*, but nourish in them a *vaine
imagination* of *immortality*, and *immutability*. But *bonum* 20
est nobis esse hic (as Saint *Peter* said there) It *is good to
dwell here*, in this *consideration* of his *death*, and therefore
transferre wee our *tabernacle* (our *devotions*) through some
of those *steps* which *God* the *Lord* made to his *issue of death*
that *day*. Take in the *whole day* from the *houre* that *Christ
received* the *passeover* upon *Thursday*, *unto* the *houre* in
which hee *died* the *next day*. Make *this* present *day* that *day*
in thy *devotion*, and consider what *hee did*, and remember
what *you have done*. Before hee *instituted* and *celebrated* the
Sacrament, (which was *after* the *eating of the passeover*) hee 30
proceeded to that *act* of *humility*, to *wash his disciples feete*,
even *Peters*, *who* for a while *resisted* him; In thy *preparation*
to the holy and blessed *Sacrament*, hast thou with a sincere
humility sought a *reconciliation* with all the *world*, even with

those that have beene *averse* from it, and *refused* that
reconciliation from thee? If so and not els thou hast spent
that *first part* of his *last day*, in a *conformity* with him. After
the *Sacrament* hee spent the time till night in *prayer*, in
preaching, in *Psalmes;* Hast thou considered that a *worthy*
receaving of the *Sacrament* consists in a *continuation* of *holi-*
nesse after, as well as in a *preparation* before? If so, thou
hast therein also *conformed* thy selfe to him, so *Christ* spent
his time till night; *At night* hee *went into the garden* to *pray*,
10 and he prayed *prolixi[o]us* he spent *much time* in *prayer*, how
much? Because it is literally expressed, that he *prayed*
there three severall times, and that *returning to his Disciples*
after his *first prayer*, and *finding them asleepe* sayd, *could ye*
not watch with me one houre, it is collected that he *spent three*
houres in *prayer*. I dare scarce aske thee *whither* thou *went-*
est, or *how* thou *disposedst* of *thy self*, when it *grew darke* and
after *last night:* If that time were spent in a *holy recom-*
mendation of thy selfe to *God*, and a *submission* of *thy will*
to *his*, It was spent in a *conformity* to him. In that *time* and
20 in those *prayers* was *his agony* and *bloody sweat*. I will *hope*
that thou didst *pray*, but not *every ordinary* and *customary*
prayer, but *prayer actually* accompanied with *shedding of*
teares, and *dispositively* in a readines to *shed blood* for *his*
glory in *necessary cases*, puts thee into a *conformity* with
him; About midnight he was *taken* and *bound with a kisse*,
art thou not *too conformable* to him in that? Is not that
too literally, too exactly *thy case?* at *midnight* to have *bene*
taken and bound with a kisse? from thence he was *caried*
back to *Jerusalem*, first to *Annas*, then to *Caiphas*, and (as
30 late as it was) then hee was *examined* and *buffeted*, and
delivered over to the custody of those *officers*, from whome
he received all those *irrisions*, and *violences*, the *covering of*
his face, the *spitting upon his face*, the *blasphemies of words*,
and the *smartnes of blowes* which that *Gospell* mentions. In

which compasse fell that *Gallicinium*, that *crowing of the Cock* which *called up Peter* to his *repentance*, how thou passedst all that time thou knowest. If thou didst any thing that needed *Peters teares*, and hast *not shed them*, let me be thy *Cock*, doe it now, Now thy *Master* (in the unworthiest of his servants) *lookes back upon thee*, doe it now; *Betimes*, in the morning, so soone as it was day, the *Jewes held a counsell* in the *high Priests hall*, and *agreed upon their evidence* against him, and then caried him to *Pilate*, who was to be his *Judge;* diddest thou *accuse* thy selfe 10 when thou *wakedst this morning*, and wast thou content even with *false accusations* (that is) rather to *suspect actions* to have beene sin, which were not, than to *smother* and *justify* such as were *truly sins?* then thou spentst that *houre* in *conformity* to him: *Pilate* found *no evidence against him*, and therefore to ease himselfe, and to passe a *complement* upon *Herod, Tetrarch* of *Galilee*, who was at that time at *Jerusalem* (because *Christ* being a *Galilean* was of *Herods jurisdiction*) *Pilat sent him* to *Herod*, and rather as a *madman* than a *malefactor, Herod* remaunded him (*with scornes*) to 20 *Pilat* to proceed against him; And this was about *eight* of the *clock*. Hast thou been content to come to this *Inquisition*, this examination, this agitation, this cribration, this pursuit of thy *conscience*, to *sift* it, to follow it from the *sinnes* of thy *youth* to thy *present sinnes*, from the *sinnes* of thy *bed*, to the *sinnes* of thy *boorde*, and from the *substance* to the *circumstance* of thy *sinnes?* That's *time spent* like thy *Saviours. Pilat* wold have *saved Christ*, by using the *priviledge* of *the day* in his behalfe, because that *day* one *prisoner was to be delivered*, but they *choose Barrabas*, hee would 30 have *saved* him *from death*, by *satisfying their fury*, with *inflicting* other *torments* upon him, *scourging* and *crowning with thornes*, and *loading* him with many *scornefull* and *ignominous contumelies;* But they regarded him not, they pressed a *crucifying*. Hast thou gone about to *redeeme thy sinne*, by *fasting*, by *Almes*, by *disciplines* and *mortifications*? in way of *satisfaction* to the *Justice* of *God?* that will not serve, that's not the right way, *wee presse* an utter *Crucifying* of that *sinne* that governes thee; and that *conformes* thee to *Christ*. Towards *noone Pilat* gave *judgement*, and they made such *hast* to execution, as that *by noone* hee was *upon the Crosse*. There now hangs that *sacred Body* upon the *Crosse*, *rebaptized* in his owne *teares* and *sweat*, and

10 *embalmed* in his *owne blood alive*. There are those *bowells of compassion*, which are so conspicuous, so manifested, as that you may *see them through his wounds*. There those *glorious eyes* grew faint in their sight: so as the *Sun ashamed* to survive them, *departed with his light too*. And then that *Sonne of God*, who was *never from us*, and yet had now come a *new way unto* us in *assuming our nature*, delivers that *soule* (which was *never out* of his *Fathers hands*) by a *new way*, a *voluntary emission* of it into his Fathers hands; For though to this *God our Lord*, *belong'd these issues of death*, so that

20 considered in his owne contract, he *must* necessarily *dye*, yet at *no breach* or *battery*, which they had made upon his *sacred Body*, issued his soule, but *emisit*, hee *gave up the Ghost*, and as *God breathed a soule into* the *first Adam*, so this *second Adam breathed his soule into God, into the hands of God*. There wee leave you in that *blessed dependancy*, to *hang* upon *him* that *hangs* upon the *Crosse*, there *bath* in his *teares*, there *suck* at his *woundes*, and *lye downe in peace* in his *grave*, till hee vouchsafe you a *resurrection*, and an *ascension* into that *Kingdome*, which hee *hath prepared for you*, with the

30 *inestimable price* of his *incorruptible blood*. AMEN.

NOTES

PAGE xvii. IZAAC WALTON. The text here given reproduces
Walton's *Life* in its first edition, 1640, when it was prefixed to
Donne's *LXXX Sermons*. In 1658 Walton issued, separately, a
'second impression corrected and enlarged'. Thereafter the
Life was issued (with the *Lives* of Wotton, Hooker, and Herbert) in 1670 and 1675. The final text, 1675, may conveniently
be consulted in the World's Classics (1927). Of the additional
matter there given, the greater part was introduced in the
edition of 1658. But an important addition in 1670 was that
of the two letters of Donne printed on pp. 36–8 of the World's
Classics text, with the paragraph immediately following; a very
moving passage. To that passage Walton added in 1675 the
story of Donne's journey to France, his 'Vision' in Paris, and
the poem *A Valediction* (World's Classics, pp. 39–44). Other
notable additions in 1675 are (1) the pretty 'John Donne, Anne
Donne, Vn-done' story (World's Classics, p. 29), and (2) Walton's account of the picture of the young Donne (the Donne of
the Marshall engraving), with the reflections suggested to him
by that picture (World's Classics, pp. 79–80). It is interesting
to observe that the really valuable additions to the 1640 text
come from 1670 and 1675 (in 1675 Walton was eighty-two).
The additions of 1658 give new information; but except for
the passage describing Donne's grief for the death of his wife
(World's Classics, pp. 51–2), they leave the ethical quality of
Walton's picture unaffected.

PAGE xlv. BEN JONSON on DONNE. l. 2. *The idea of a woman*: see Donne's letter to G. G., printed on p. 79.

l. 5. *the Lost Chaine*: Elegie xi (O.P.* pp. 85–9).

l. 6. *the calme*: The second poem of the *Letters to Severall
Personages* (O.P. pp. 157–8).

PAGE xlv. DRUMMOND OF HAWTHORNDEN ON DONNE. l. 15.
Alexander's: Sir William Alexander, Earl of Stirling 1567 ?–
1640, a friend of Drummond's; dramatist and sonneteer. Drummond is speaking of the sonnets in Alexander's *Aurora, con-
taining the first fancies of the Author's youth*, 1604.

l. 21. *Marry and Love*: Donne's second Elegy, which begins
with these words (O.P. p. 72).

Tasso's Stanzas: Stanze sopra la Bellezza.

* O.P. = The Oxford Poets edition of *The Poems of John Donne*,
ed. H. J. C. Grierson (1929).

PAGE xlv. DRYDEN ON DONNE.

(a) l. 23. *catachresis*: forced phraseology.

PAGE xlvi. 4. *Cleveland's*: John Cleveland, 1613-58, royalist, poet, and satirist, a contemporary of Milton's at Christ's College, Cambridge; fellow of St. John's, 1634-45. In 1647 he published *Several School Poems*. In 1655 he was imprisoned, but after a short time released by Cromwell. In the year following appeared his *Poems*. His works were collected after his death in a volume entitled *Clievelandi Vindiciae*, 1677.

(b) The Earl of Dorset to whom Dryden addressed his Essay was Charles Sackville, 1638-1706, sixth Earl of Dorset and first Earl of Middlesex. Not content with putting Dorset at the head of Satire ('your lordship in satire, and Shakespeare in tragedy'), Dryden wrote to him: 'Your Lyric Poems are the delight and wonder of this age, and will be the envy of the next' (*Works*, xiii. 5). Johnson, deprecating these extravagances (in his *Life* of Dorset), is content (in his *Life* of Cowley) to borrow Dryden's criticisms of Donne, blaming his 'metaphysics', his 'numbers', his 'expression', and his gift of exciting admiration without affording delight (see Note on *Valediction, forbidding mourning*, p. 110).

PAGE xlvii. *Robert Wolseley*: In 1685 he published (anonymously) a Preface to *Valentinian, a Tragedy, As 'tis Altered by the late Earl of Rochester, and Acted at the Theatre-Royal*. The *Preface* contends that morality and art have nothing to do with one another; a thesis which is handled with immense cleverness, giving the essay a place of the first importance in seventeenth-century criticism.

PAGE xlvii. COLERIDGE ON DONNE. (c) The Note was jotted down by Coleridge in a copy of Chalmers's *English Poets* (not his own, but that of his Highgate host, Gillman). We find him, similarly, making Notes in a copy of Donne belonging to Lamb (Lamb, *Letters*, 1935, p. 382); it is likely that, like Hazlitt, he had no copy of his own. 'The verses', H. N. Coleridge wrote, 'were added in pencil to the collection of commendatory lines [at the end of Donne's Poems]. No. i is Mr Coleridge's; the publication of No. ii, I trust the all-accomplished author will, under the circumstances, pardon.' I do not know who the 'all-accomplished author' was—it is not clear that H. N. Coleridge knew.

PAGE xlviii. 4. *Aretine*: Pietro of Arezzo, 1492-1556, tragedian, comedian, satirist, sonneteer, celebrated for the ribaldry of his compositions. 'I am sory', writes Donne to Sir Henry Wotton, 'you should (with any great earnestness) desyre any thing of P. Aretinus, not that he could infect; but that it seemes you are already infected with the common opinion of him: beleeve me

he is much lesse than his fame and was too well payd by the
Roman church in that coyne which he coveted most where his
bookes were by the counsell of Trent forbidden which if they
had beene permitted to have beene worne by all long ere this
had beene worne out: his divinyty was but a sirrope to enwrapp
his prophane bookes to get them passage, yet in these bookes
which have devine titles there is least harme as in his letters
most good; his others have no other singularyty in them but
that they are forbidden' (Burley MS.). Aretinus comes in for
further censure in *Ignatius his Conclave* (Hayward, p. 391), and,
again, in Satyre iv. 70 (O.P. p. 143). In Milton's *Areopagitica* he
is spoken of, among those writers who have acquainted Princes
'with the choicest delights, and criticisms of sin', as 'that
notorious ribald of Arezzo' (*Works*, Columbia Press, iv. 313).

PAGE xlviii. HAZLITT ON DONNE. In the 'Lectures on the English Poets' (iv, *ad fin.*) Hazlitt confesses that he 'knows nothing'
of Donne outside the *Valediction, forbidding mourning* and 'some
quaint riddles in verse which the Sphinx could not unravel'.
This was in 1818; and he repeats it in 1819. In 1819, however,
he published *The English Comic Writers*, where Donne occupies
a considerable section of chapter iii. Hazlitt's criticisms of
Donne repeat, in general, those of Johnson and Dryden—he
wrote, it is clear, when he was fresh from reading Johnson's
Life of Cowley. That his reading of Donne had been hurried
and perfunctory seems certain. He speaks of the Satires as too
'clerical',—as though they had been written by the Dean of St.
Paul's. He supposes *The Funeral* to have been written after the
death of Donne's wife. He speaks of the *Epithalamion* of 1613
as celebrating the nuptials of 'a Count Palatine of the Rhine';
the reader would scarcely guess that the person spoken of was
Frederick, Prince Palatine, King of Bohemia and son-in-law of
King James I. Nowhere, whether praising Donne or disparaging
him, is he vital or convincing or characteristic. His last paragraph is his worst—he cannot, it seems, forget (what some of
us find it difficult to remember) that Donne was a clergyman.

PAGE 3. SONG. 'SWEETEST LOVE. . . .' Called by Coleridge
'This beautiful and perfect poem' (*Notes, Theological, Political,
and Miscellaneous*, p. 250).

PAGE 5. THE GOOD-MORROW.

l. 4. *seaven sleepers*: the Seven Sleepers of Ephesus, seven
youths who, walled up in a cave by the persecuting Emperor
Decius, slept miraculously for 187 days. See Gibbon, *Decline
and Fall*, ch. 33.

PAGE 6. BREAK OF DAYE. (*a*) appears first in 1612: in that
year, it is printed, with the signature 'J. D.', in John Dowland's

Pilgrim's Solace; and again, in Orlando Gibbons's *XVI Madrigals and Mottets*. In the 1665 edition of Donne's *Poems* it appears as the first stanza of a poem of which (*b*) furnishes stanzas ii–iv; so too in two of our MSS. (added, in one of them, however, by a different hand). That the two pieces are not part of one and the same poem seems sufficiently indicated by the metre. That (*b*) is spoken in the person of a woman appears from the last stanza, and from the last line of the stanza preceding.

PAGE 7. THE ECSTASIE. 'I would never find fault with metaphysical poems, were they all like this, or but half as excellent', Coleridge, *Notes*, &c., p. 255.

PAGE 10. A FEAVER. ll. 27–8. Coleridge, quoting these two lines, speaks of them as 'just and affecting'. But 'All the preceding verses', he adds, 'are detestable' (*Notes*, &c., p. 254) —it is difficult to think that, so speaking, he had read the first stanza.

PAGE 10. A VALEDICTION: FORBIDDING MOURNING. In the 1675 edition of his *Life* of Donne, but not in the earlier editions, Walton prints this poem as 'a Copy of Verses given by Mr Donne to his wife at the time that he then [in 1611] parted from her'. The occasion was his visit to France with Sir Robert Drury. 'And I beg leave to tell', Walton adds, 'that I have heard some critics, learned both in Languages and poetry, say, that none of the Greek or Latine Poets did ever equal them' (*Life*, World's Classics, p. 42). 'An admirable poem', Coleridge says, 'which none but Donne could have written. Nothing was ever more admirably made than the figure of the compass' (*Notes*, &c., p. 355). It is interesting to compare Dr. Johnson's comment: 'To the . . . comparison of a man that travels and his wife that stays at home with a pair of compasses, it may be doubted whether absurdity or ingenuity has the better claim.' 'It is apparent', he adds, 'that whatever is improper or vicious is produced by a voluntary deviation from nature in pursuit of something new and strange, and that the ['metaphysical'] writers fail to give delight by their desire of exciting admiration' (*Lives of the Poets*, Oxford, 1905, i, pp. 34–5).

PAGE 11. THE BAITE. The title is not given in the first edition of Donne's *Poems*, but appears in all editions from 1635 to 1669. One of our MSS. has, for title, 'An invitation to his Mrs. to come and fish'. It is worth noting that, close friend as he was to the author of *The Compleat Angler*, Donne regarded fishermen as an 'unkinde kinde', and disliked 'Fasts and Lents' because of the 'rape' of fish involved; see *The Progresse of the*

Soule, 281–90 (O.P. p. 279). The poem, one among a number of imitations of Marlowe's 'Come live with me . . .' (which Shakespeare thought fit to quote in the *Merry Wives*, III. i. 17–26), is printed by Walton in his *Compleat Angler*, 1653, 'to show the world that *Donne* could make soft and smooth verses, when he thought them fit and worth his while' (ch. xii).

PAGE 12. WOMANS CONSTANCY. Coleridge's comment upon this poem is adequate: 'After all there is but one Donne' (*Notes, &c.*, p. 251).

PAGE 13. 11–13: or, in order to justifie your own end, in purposing change and falsehood, (will you say that) you can have no way to be true except falsehood?

PAGE 13. THE SUNNE RISING. A poem characterized, says Coleridge, by 'true vigorous exultation, both soul and body in full puissance' (*Notes, &c.*, p. 252).

l. 17. *both the'Indias*: the East Indies, famous for their spices, and the West Indies, famous for their gold-mines. In stanza ii of *The Progresse of the Soule* we have similarly the 'first east' and 'Iland spices there' (3–4) contrasted with the 'Westerne land of Myne' (7). The use of 'Myne' for mines of gold, silver, and precious minerals seems to be peculiar to Donne (Coleridge, *Literary Remains*, i, p. 150).

PAGE 14. 21. *I*: Ay (as in Elegy vii. 14); unless, with Chambers, we punctuate 'Princes I.'

ll. 25–6. The Sun, which has to traverse the world from east to west, is less happy than the two lovers who have the whole world with them contracted to the narrow space where they lie.

PAGE 14. THE INDIFFERENT. l. 17. *travaile thorow you*: journey through you, as through a land in which I am only a tourist.

PAGE 15. 26–7. The sense would be given by the punctuation

> But I have told them 'Since you will be true,
> You shall be true to them who are false to you'.

The 'you' is part of Venus' address to the 'two or three Poor Heretiques in love' who believe in constancy.

PAGE 15. THE CANONIZATION. 'One of my favourite poems', Coleridge, *Notes, &c.*, p. 249.

ll. 7–8. Be a courtier, or be a money-maker.

l. 15. *the plaguie Bill*: the list of casualties from the Plague; see Elegy xiv. 2:

> I ask'd the number of the Plaguy Bill.   (O.P. p. 95.)

'Bills' of mortality from the Plague can be traced back in London to 1519. In Donne's time they were issued weekly, during periods of epidemic. Of written bills examples are extant, in the sixteenth century, from the years 1535 and 1582.

Printed bills began to be issued, it is probable, in 1592. Donne's references connect, it seems likely, with the years 1592–3; one of the worst periods. Other bad Plague years in Donne's life-time were 1582–3, 1603, 1625. See F. P. Wilson, *The Plague in Shakespeare's London*, pp. 76–9, 189–201.

PAGE 16. 20. *flye*: i.e. insignificant creature; as Chaucer, *Reeve's Tale*, 272, 'I count him nat a flye'. But Donne has in mind, as appears from the next line, the taper-fly (see Drum-mond, *Poems*, ed. Kastner, i, p. 71, Song II. 208, 'And like the taper-fly, there burn thy wings').

l. 23. *The Phoenix ridle*: Donne's Phoenix is not the classical Phoenix, the Phoenix of Lactantius Firmianus, 'quae Veneris foedera nulla coit', but the more romantic creature whose mis-cellaneous fame is illustrated in Robert Chester's *Loves Martyr*, 1601, with its appendix of 'Diverse Poeticall Essaies'—among them, Shakespeare's *Phoenix and Turtle*. It is difficult not to think that Donne had in mind Shakespeare's

> So they loved, as love in twain
> Had the essence but in one;
> Two distincts, division none:
> Number there in love was slain.

The Dove of 22 is the turtle-dove; the Eagle, in the same line, perhaps typifies constancy, as in Chester's *Meeting Dialogue-wise between Nature, the Phoenix and the Turtle Dove*—

> But those that have true perfect constant eyes
> She cherishes, the rest she doth despise

(ed. Grosart, New Shakespeare Society, 1878, p. 119). See Note on *An Epithalamion, or Marriage Song*, pp. 116–17.

l. 28. *it*: love.

l. 39. *now*: since your canonization, since you ceased to move among men.

ll. 40–5. You who did contract into yourselves the soul of the whole world, and throw it on the mirror of your eyes, making them such mirrors, such spies, that they gave you every-thing in epitome, counties, towns, courts: [we, your worship-pers, pray you to] petition heaven for us to give us a pattern, i.e. a copy, of your love.

With 40 'did the whole worlds soule contract', we may com-pare *The Sunne Rising*, 26, 'the world's contracted thus', where, similarly, the meaning is that all that the sun surveys, all states and princes, everything in the world that is interesting, meets contracted into one narrow space where lovers are.

PAGE 17. THE TRIPLE FOOLE. l. 5. If only his mistress favoured him.

l. 16. Coleridge calls the line 'A good instance how Donne read his verses. We should write, "The grief, verse did restraine"; but Donne rightly emphasised the two main words, Grief and Verse, and therefore made each the first syllable of a trochee or dactyl—

Grief, which/ verse did re/strain'

(*Notes*, &c., p. 250).

ll. 17–18. Love and Grief deserve to be versified, but not in verse which is read aloud (or sung).

PAGE 17. THE ANNIVERSARIE. l. 4. *Is*: the singular verb has for its subject, not merely the neighbouring singulars 'The Sun' and 'All glory', but the remoter plurals 'All Kings, &c. . . .'

PAGE 18. 25. *Who is so safe as wee?* The words suggested to Rupert Brooke what is perhaps the finest of his sonnets, the second of the War Sonnets of 1914:

Dear, of all happy in the hour, most blest
He who has found our hid security,
Assured in the dark tides of the world at rest,
And heard our word, *Who is so safe as we?* . . .

PAGE 18. TWICKNAM GARDEN. Twickenham Park was the residence of Donne's friend the Countess of Bedford; to whom, in one of his verse-Letters, he says:

The story of beauty,'in Twickenham is, and you.
Who hath seen one, would both

(O.P. p. 170, ll. 70–1).

l. 1. Gosse calls the line 'one of *Donne's* most famous traps for the ear'; scanning it

Blasted/ with sighs/ and/ surrounded/ with tears.

But the Notes of one of Donne's contemporaries, Giles Oldisworth, scans

Blast*ed with* sighs, and surround*ed with* teares,

taking the first two feet, and the last two, as choriambs substituted for double iambi ($- \cup \cup -$ for $\cup - \cup -$). It is Gosse who has fallen into the trap. (See John Sampson, *Contemporary Light upon John Donne*, in *Essays and Studies*, vii, p. 87.)

PAGE 19. A VALEDICTION: OF THE BOOKE. l. 3. *Esloygne*: send far off (French *éloigner*).

l. 7. *her*: Corinna, a Boeotian poetess of Tanagra, who won a victory over the Theban Pindar; Pausanias says that her victory was due as much to her beauty as to her poetic gift (9. 22. 3).

l. 8. *her, through whose helpe*: Polla Argentaria, Lucan's wife; Sidonius Apollinaris, *Epp.* 2. 10. 6.

l. 9. *her, whose booke*: Phantasia, a mythical Egyptian poetess, daughter of Nicarchus of Memphis. She wrote an *Iliad* and an *Odyssey*, depositing both in the temple of Hephaestus in her native Memphis; whence Homer procured a copy. So Photius; whose *Bibliotheca* was translated into Latin in 1606.

PAGE 20. 19–26: The syntactical difficulties are removed, if, as I have ventured to do, we place line 22 in parentheses; all our texts show merely a comma after *Idiome* and a colon after *instruments*. When this book of our letters to one another— which shall live as long as the world—written in the cipher and idiom of poetry (we, in making it, are merely instruments of the learned in love), when this book is thus made, Learning will be safe against the Vandals and Goths.

PAGE 21. A NOCTURNALL. The Feast of St. Lucia, Virgin and Martyr, falls on 23 December, by Gregorian reckoning; corresponding with 13 December by the Julian calendar, which Donne used. In no year during the period of Donne's lifetime was this day, astronomically, 'the shortest day'. To find a year in which the Feast of St. Lucia coincided with the shortest day, we have to go back to the year 1487 (I owe this information to the kindness of Professor Plaskett).

With this gloomy and somewhat obscure poem may be compared *The Dissolution* (O.P. pp. 57–8). The two pieces may be plausibly conjectured to lament the death of one and the same person—if a real person, we do not know who she was. It has been suggested that the *Nocturnall* was written for Lucie, Countess of Bedford, on the occasion of an illness (in 1612) so severe that Donne speaks of her as already dead—using, incidentally, language which suggests that she had been his mistress. The sole support for this suggestion seems to be that the Countess bore the same name as the Saint.

PAGE 22. 7 ? Life has shrunk into the earth, like a going-to-bed.

l. 14. *expresse*: squeeze out; a Latinism. Love squeezed a refined essence even out of unessential being, nothingness.

l. 29. The quintessence of primordial nothingness.

ll. 34–6. All things have some property or other; if I were the usual kind of nothing, e.g. a shadow, there would be some light and some body to make the shadow.

PAGE 23. 39. *The Goat*: Capricorn; as in the *First Anniversarie*, 265. The Sun enters Capricorn *c.* 22 December, but by the Old Style, which Donne uses, 10 days earlier.

PAGE 25. THE WILL. The ingenuity of the bequests deserves analysis. Donne divides his gifts and possessions among five classes: (1) those who have too much of what is given; (2) those who have too little or nothing; (3) those who will take what is given as an insult; (4) those to whom he merely restores what they gave him; (5) those to whom what is given will come too late to be of any use to them. Only towards the fourth class does he show real generosity, and only, here, to some members of the class—he is sensible that he owes his reputation to his friends, his wit to the company in which he exercised it, his poetry to 'Nature' (unnatural stuff though many have thought it to be): to the doctors he is in debt for sickness, to the philosophers for doubt. The final stanza nullifies, by a crowning paradox, all that has preceded. By dying, he will undo his own gifts; his death will mean that love dies, and the death of love will mean the death of all the world, to say nothing of himself, of his mistress, of the God of Love.

Stanza iii is absent from a good many of our MSS., and is probably a later addition; it appears in all our printed texts, from 1633 on. It might be thought safe, perhaps, in 1633, and not in 1603.

l. 12. *ingenuity*: ingenuousness. The *O.E.D.* quotes Raleigh and Selden, both 1614, for the same use.

l. 23. *bare*: bare of modesty.   *

PAGE 26. 40. *brazen medals*: Donne would seem to mean war-decorations, which he thinks a poor consolation for indigent ex-soldiers. In this country, the earliest war-medals are the Armada medals of 1588–9. For the reign of James I no such medals are extant. Of the word *medal*, as war-decoration, this is perhaps the earliest use in English, though the passage is not noted by the *O.E.D.*

PAGE 27. THE FUNERAL. Grierson, and others, suppose that this poem, *The Blossome*, *The Relique*, and (not here printed) *The Primrose* (O.P. pp. 54–5), perhaps even *The Dampe* (O.P. p. 57), were 'addressed to Mrs Herbert in the earlier days of Donne's intimacy with her in Oxford or London'. With the bracelet of hair in line 3, and in *The Relique*, line 6, he compares the bracelet of hair given by Stelliana (Lady Venetia Stanley) to Theagenes (Sir Kenelm Digby, 1603–65) (Digby, *Private Memoirs*, pp. 80–1). These poems occur juxtaposed in our printed texts, and in some of our MSS. Except that *The Primrose* was written at Montgomery Castle, the seat of the Herbert family, there seems, in fact, to be nothing to connect any of them with Mrs. Herbert (nor is *The Primrose* addressed to her, nor about her). From the fact that St. Mary Magdalen is mentioned in *The Relique*, 17, and that Mrs. Herbert bore the name Magdalen, it seems hardly possible to draw any inference. Two poems certainly addressed to Mrs. Herbert are *The Autumnal* (O.P. pp. 83–4), and the sonnet beginning 'Her of your name ...' (O.P. p. 288); *almost* certainly addressed to her are the lines beginning 'Mad paper stay . . .' (pp. 48–50). There is nothing in anything which Donne certainly wrote to her that suggests a relation 'romantic' or 'lover-like'; and to connect with her *any* of the *Songs and Sonets* seems speculative and idle. Of Donne's relations with Mrs. Herbert, Walton, in his *Life* of Donne, says nothing. But in his *Life* of George Herbert, Mrs. Herbert's son, he has a good deal to say on the subject. The 'amity' between them, he writes, 'was not an *Amity* that polluted their Souls; but an *Amity* made up of a chain of sutable inclinations and vertues; an *Amity* like that of *St. Chrysostoms* to his dear and vertuous *Olympias* . . . Or, an *Amity* indeed more like that of *St Hierom* to his *Paula* . . .' (World's Classics, p. 265). Walton had 'many of their letters', and was in a position, he says, to give 'more demonstrations of the Friendship, and many sacred Indearments betwixt these two excellent persons' (ib., p. 267). Walton knew what he was talking about—and what not to talk about.

PAGE 33. ELEGY v. ll. 14–16. Do his wounds affect me? do they make him, that is, think me of less worth? do they impair his judgement, so that he now looks on me with less loving eyes?

l. 20. *that which*: the *which* seems metrically redundant. Was it inserted by Donne's first editor (1633) to explain *that* (*that* used for *what*)?

PAGE 34. ELEGY xii. l. 7. Should the Moon and all the stars leave Venus alone.

l. 9. *thee*: Venus.

l. 19. *Right*: i.e. Rite, as in *Secona Anniversary*, 119 (p. 57).

l. 30. *Dove-like*: see *The Canonization*, 23, note.

PAGE 35. 42. *the husbands towred eyes*: the eyes of a husband who eyes us as from a watch-tower. This is the reading of the Harleian MS. 4064. Our printed texts have 'thy husbands towring eyes' (Norton takes *towring* as a misprint for *lowering*). It is difficult to think that 'thy' is right—Donne is addressing, not his mistress, but the God of Love. The Bodleian MS. Rawlinson 31, like the Harleian MS., has 'the'.

l. 43. 'Inflam'd with th'oughlie' (i.e. ugly), the printed texts: the MSS. have 'That flame with oylie'.

l. 54. *thy*: he is still addressing the God of Love whose innermost parts, and 'panting heart' the lovers have penetrated. But the expressions employed are crude and obscure. 'I can make no sense of the line . . . as it stands', says Grierson. The Harleian MS., and some others, have 'Yea, thy pale colours inward as thy heart?' But this looks very much like free emendation.

PAGE 37. AN EPITHALAMION, OR MARRIAGE SONG. The poem

celebrates the nuptials of Elizabeth, daughter of James I, and Frederick, Elector Palatine, later King of Bohemia. The wedding took place on 14 Feb. 1613. The bride and bridegroom, figured as 'two Phoenixes', follow the fashion set, in 1601, by *Love's Martyr* (see Note, p. 112).

There are extant two letters of Donne to the Queen of Bohemia (Oct. 1622, Feb. 1624). The first of them accompanied a copy of Donne's first printed Sermon, the second was written 'upon presentation of a Book of Meditations' (i.e. the *Devotions upon Emergent Occasions*). In acknowledging the second of these two gifts the Queen writes to Donne that she 'never did but with delight' listen to his Sermons. It would be interesting to know whether she ever read this frank and pagan *Epithalamion*. When he wrote it, Donne was contemplating taking orders.

PAGE 41. EPITHALAMION MADE AT LINCOLNES INNE. Of the occasion, and persons concerned, nothing is known. The poem may be assigned with probability to the period during which Donne was studying law at Lincoln's Inn; the Bridegroom would seem to be a student of the Inn (29–31). The rhythm of one or two of the lines (e.g. 25, 66) sorts with an early date of composition; so does the bad rhyme *cradle, able* in lines 80–81.

l. 16. *Thousands of Angels*: gold angels, or nobles; the same pun runs, tiresomely, all through Elegy xi.

PAGE 42. 54–8. The sun still sweats, in our hemisphere (for it is the summer season). He moves swiftly in winter (taking, at the solstice, 7¾ hours for his whole journey). But at the moment he is stationary, though he shadows (throws a shadow indicating) his turning. (Cf. Epistle of St. James, i. 17, 'the Father of lights with whom is no . . . shadow of turning'.) He has reached noon (his turning-point); his steeds for the moment will go slow, but quicken ('gallop lively') as he descends to the west. When he has run the other half of his course, you shall put on perfection.

This paraphrase suggests that in line 57 the *nill* of one of our MSS. (adopted by Grierson for the *will* of all our other texts) is not more than a clever emendation.

l. 56. *shadowes*: not a substantive, but a verb; the subject is the sun.

PAGE 44. SATYRE iii. 'If you would teach a scholar in the highest forms to *read*, take Donne, and of Donne this satire': Coleridge, *Notes*, &c., p. 250.

The poem may be called a Defence of Philosophic Doubt; but with an important qualification. What Donne is in doubt about is not the Christian religion, but the true form of that religion—whether truth is to be sought in Rome, Geneva, or London. In a letter to Sir Henry Goodyere (printed in Gosse, ii, pp. 77–80) he speaks of 'that true sound opinion that in all Christian professions there is a way to salvation'. 'The channels of God's mercies', he there says, 'run through both fields' (the Roman and the Puritan). In another letter, addressed to 'Sir H. R.', but probably written to Goodyere, 'You know,' he writes, 'I have never imprisoned the word Religion . . . immuring it in a Rome or a Geneva; they are all virtual beams of one Sun' (*Letters*, 1651, p. 29; cited by Grierson, ii, p. 115). The date of these two letters is uncertain; they may be assigned, plausibly, to some date between 1608 and 1614. But the liberal temper which they evince was with Donne to the end. It makes its first decisive appearance in the third Satire. To how early a date the third Satire belongs we do not know certainly. One of our MSS. assigns it (with Satires i and ii) to 1593. Such historical allusions as occur in it do not much help. The English (Sidney among them) were giving aid to the 'mutinous Dutch' (17) in 1586. What is said of 'frozen North discoveries' (22) suggests the attempts of John Davis to find the north-west passage in three successive years, 1585–7. But Donne may conceivably be thinking of the voyages of the Dutchman Barents in 1594. The sonnet *To Mr. C. B.* (O.P. p. 184) suggests that Donne himself at some time entertained the idea of exploring northern regions 'where sterne winter age doth wonne'. The 'fires of Spain and the line' call up Donne's own adventures in Cadiz and the Azores in 1596–7. But it is perhaps more likely that he is thinking of earlier adventurers in the tropic regions. What is said in the concluding lines of the poem about the encroachment of 'mans lawes' on the conscience may look back to the Recusancy laws of 1582, or the operations of the Court of High Commission in 1583; or, again, it may be purely general, and may take in other countries than England. It might have been said equally well, and feelingly, by a Calvinist or a Catholic. What Donne believed when he wrote this Satire, nothing tells us: 'glib conjecture', Gosse says, properly, 'is here all out of place'.

l. 1. *spleene*: for the spleen as the seat of the faculty of ridicule, see the poem [of Donne] cited by Gosse, i, p. 82.

> Nothing whereat to laugh my spleen essays.

Hall, similarly, perhaps a little earlier, has (Sat. IV. i. 74)

> Now laugh I loud and break my spleen . . .

ll. 5–11. Does not Religion deserve the same loyalty from us that Virtue had from the pagans? Is not the prospect of being rewarded by everlasting joys in heaven as powerful with us to calm our lusts as the prospect of being honoured on earth for Virtue was with the pagans ('to them'=to the people of 'the blinded age'—Donne thinks of the Greeks and Romans in particular). Alas, shall we, when we surpass the pagans in the means to salvation (Christian faith), allow them to get the better of us in *attaining* salvation ('in the end')? Shall your father, in the next world, meet pagans accepted for the goodness of their lives—their goodness counted for faith—and hear you damned, after he taught you the easy way to salvation?

l. 24. *Children in th'oven*: see the poem *The Calme*, 28,

> Where walkers in hot Ovens do not die

(O.P. p. 158).

The reference in both passages is to Shadrach, Meshach, and Abednego in Daniel, iii. 20–30.

the line: the Equator. See *To Sir Henry Wotton*, 11, 'the furnace of the even line' (O.P. p. 160).

l. 28. *thy*: we should expect *his*. But the sense is given by *Or 'eate thy poysonous words'*, i.e. Or have 'eate thy poysonous words' shouted at him.

ll. 33–5. Know thy foes (hate and fight the Devil); in return for your hate (but not for your love) the Devil will be fain to forfeit his whole kingdom (to let it be quittance for a stubborn resistance to him). To hate the Devil is the way to dispossess him.

PAGE 45. 49. *Crates*: this is the reading of one of our MSS. The printed texts have *Crants* or *Grants*. *Crates* matches the other proper names, all Greek-derived. (In 43 *Mirreus=Myrrheus*, the name chosen for its suggestion of femininity: with this is contrasted *Crates*, from *kratos*, strength.)

ll. 69–73. You have got to accept one or other of these forms of religion. You can choose for yourself ('unmoved of force', 69), or you can accept a form dictated to you. You can ask your father which is the true form—and he ask his. Falsehood came into the world almost with Truth; Truth is even so a little older. It is worth while, enquiring, to go back in time. The great thing is, to enquire.

PAGE 46. 82. And so reach that which the sudden (i.e. unexpected) hill resists approach to.

l. 96. *Philip*: Philip II of Spain.

Gregory: ? Pope Gregory XIII, the Pope of Donne's boyhood —he died in 1585. But Donne may mean some more distant Gregory—Gregory the Great, or Gregory VII.

l. 97. *Harry*: Henry VIII.

Martin: ? Pope Martin V; who in 1418 asserted the doctrine of Papal infallibility. Editors generally seem to suppose Donne to mean Martin Luther; just as some of them take *Philip* in 96 as Melanchthon.

PAGE 47. TO SIR HENRY GOODYERE. Sir Henry Goodyere, 1571–1627, of Polesworth in Warwickshire, gentleman of the privy chamber to James I, was over a long period one of Donne's best and closest friends. At one time Donne wrote him a weekly letter. A part of this correspondence was printed in the *Letters* of 1651: Gosse's *Life* of Donne brings together between forty and fifty letters. Like Donne, he contributed verses to Coryat's *Crudities* in 1611, and to the collection of Elegies on Prince Henry printed in 1613 in Sylvester's *Lachrymae Lachrymarum*. His uncle, of the same name, was the patron of Michael Drayton. To the nephew Drayton addressed an Ode, Ben Jonson a twelve-line epigram. Camden has preserved for us an epitaph of Goodyere, written, it is conjectured, by a kinsman, William Goodyere:

> An ill year of a Goodyere us bereft,
> Who gone to God much lack of him here left;
> Full of good gifts, of body and of mind,
> Wise, comely, learned, eloquent and kind.

It is not clear whether the 'him' of line 2 is God or Goodyere— it is probably the former. The epitaph is, at least, 'eloquent and kind'.

This is Donne's only verse-letter to Goodyere. His verse-letters, in general, may well be thought the least successful of his compositions: this and that to *M. H. H.* may pass for two of the better ones.

PAGE 49. To M. H. H. For '*M. H. H.*' one of our MSS. has 'Mrs. M. H. H.'; and it is generally accepted that the person addressed is Mrs. Herbert. For Donne's relations with her, see the introductory note to *The Funerall*.

PAGE 50. 38. *sav'd*: kept, not thrown away. But 'sav'd' also in the religious sense, as attaining heavenly happiness.

l. 43. *the same that they protest*: what they say she does.

ll. 46–7. *Marke, if her Oathes . . . Reserv'd*: note whether, in her vows never to marry again, she does not make a reservation in his case. The person alluded to throughout lines 37–52 is no doubt Sir John Danvers, Mrs. Herbert's second husband, whom she married in 1608.

PAGE 51. FROM THE FIRST ANNIVERSARY. The two *Anniversaries* are the only poems of Donne published by himself (the Elegy on Prince Henry and the verses on Coryat's *Crudities* belong to books to which he is merely part-contributor). The first of them appeared in 1611 under the title *An Anatomy of the World. Wherein, By occasion of the untimely death of Mistris Elizabeth Drvry, the frailty and the decay of this whole World is represented.* This was followed in 1612 by *The first Anniversarie. An Anatomie of the World. Wherein*, &c. *The second Anniversarie. Of the Progres of the Soule. Wherein*, &c.

Elizabeth Drury, daughter of Donne's patron, Sir Robert Drury, of Hawsted, Suff., died in 1610. Elizabeth Drury Donne had never seen; whether, when he wrote the first *Anniversary*, he knew the father is not certain. He was with the father in France in 1611–12, when the second *Anniversary* was written. Elegies upon persons wholly unknown to the poet were not unknown in the seventeenth century. Both Donne and Beaumont wrote Elegies on Lady Marckham (for Donne's see O.P. p. 254), but 'I never saw thy face' Beaumont says frankly.

For Ben Jonson's criticism of these poems, and Donne's excuses, see pp. xliv–v. For other excuses, put less effectively, see Donne's letter to G. G., p. 79. Coleridge copies out a part of this letter, and comments 'To be sure, these Anniversaries were the strangest caprice of genius upon record' (*Notes*, &c., p. 259).

PAGE 54. 464–5. The song is that given in the penultimate chapter of Deuteronomy. Deuteronomy and Leviticus furnish the Law, Genesis, Exodus, and Numbers the History; the Prophets, in Moses' time, were still to come.

PAGE 60. ELEGIE ON M^{RIS}. BOULSTRED. 'Cecil Bulstrode, daughter of Edward Bulstrode of Hedgerley Bulstrode, Bucks, was baptized at Beaconsfield, Feb. 12, 1583–4. She died at the house of her kinswoman, Lady Bedford, at Twickenham on August 4, 1609' (Chambers, ii, p. 230). She is probably the person commemorated in the poem to Lady Bedford, 'You that are she and you . . .' (O.P. pp. 204–5). Ben Jonson wrote on her, while she lived, a scurrilous 'Epigram' (*Underwoods*, xlix). But this did not prevent him, when she died, celebrating her virtues in an epitaph extravagant and servile. See Simpson, *Ben Jonson*, i. 59, ii. 356. It is worth noting that of Donne's seven 'Epicedes and Obsequies' three were written for kin of the Countess of Bedford, Mrs. Boulstred, Lady Marckham, Lord Harrington—all of them died in her house.

PAGE 62. THE PROGRESSE OF THE SOULE. Donne prefixed to the poem a Dedication, and a date: 'Infinitati Sacrum. 10. Augusti 1601.' In stanza 5 he speaks of himself as not far from thirty years old; and unless the Book of Destiny, he says, has another thirty years of life in store for him, it is not worth his while to begin his poem. The poem is to be a long one; tracing the history of the Soul from Adam and Eve to Queen Elizabeth, beginning in the Garden of Eden and ending on the banks of the Thames. He never carried it beyond the 'first song', 52 stanzas; the Soul is still in the near neighbourhood of Eden when he ends. He called his poem 'poema satyricon'. Ben Jonson, in 1619, gave this account of it to Drummond: 'The conceit of Dones Transformation or μετεμψύχοσις was that he sought the soule of that Aple which Eve pulled and thereafter made it the soule of a Bitch, then of a sheewolf, & so of a woman. his generall purpose was to have brought in all the bodies of the Hereticks from ye soule of Cain & at last left it in ye body of Calvin. Of this he never wrotte but one sheet, & now since he was made Doctor repenteth highlie & seeketh to destroy all his poems.' Grierson, and editors generally, suppose Jonson to be 'recalling the poem somewhat inaccurately . . . for it is evident that in [Donne's] first intention Queen Elizabeth herself [and not Calvin] was to be the soul's last host'. Jonson can be recalling, in any case, not the poem (beyond the 'first song'), but Donne's account of it. He may be supposed to mean, not that the soul found its last home in Calvin, but that Calvin was the last *heretic* in whom it lodged. Thereafter it passed to Queen Elizabeth. That Donne conceived Elizabeth as a heretic, and that his purpose in the poem was to satirize her, seems in itself unlikely, and to be contradicted by the lofty and earnest strain of stanza vii. Yet both Grierson and Gosse suppose that the poem was intended to culminate in an exposure of Elizabeth as 'the great tyrannical persecutor of the Catholics' (Gosse, i. 135). It is worth recalling that in his *Sermons*—though the earliest of these belong to a much later date—Donne speaks of Calvin with invariable respect. For what he has to say of Elizabeth, see *XXVI Sermons*, p. 354 (printed on pp. 82–6).

IV. 31. *Commissary*: See *To Sr Henry Wotton* (O.P. p. 165), 10–11, 'rugged Fate, God's Commissary'.

PAGE 63. VI. 55. *light, and light*: 'The two senses of *Light* are opposed to different opposites,' Lamb, *Letters*, iv, p. 421, 1935 (where he calls the *Metempsychosis* 'this admirable poem').

PAGE 64. VIII. 77. *the selfe same roome*: see *Hymne to God my God, in my sicknesse*, 21–2,

> We thinke that *Paradise* and *Calvarie*,
> *Christs* Crosse, and *Adams* tree, stood in one place.

X. 91–2. See *The first Anniversary*, 106–7,

> One woman at one blow, then kill'd us all,
> And singly, one by one, they kill us now.

PAGE 70. BIATHANATOS. The *Biathanatos*, written between 1602 and 1609, was licensed for publication in 1644, entered at Stationers' Hall 1646, and published (undated) in 1647. The title-page advertises it as 'A Declaration of that Paradoxe, or Thesis, that Selfe-homicide is not so Naturally Sinne, that it may never be otherwise'. 'It was written,' Donne says, in a letter to Sir Robert Carr in 1619, 'many years since; and because it is upon a misinterpretable subject, I have always gone so near suppressing it, as that it is onely not burnt . . . onely to some particular friends in both Universities, then when I writ it, I did communicate it.' One of these 'particular friends' was Herbert of Cherbury; in 1642 Herbert gave his manuscript copy of it to the Bodleian, where it now is. 'A book written by Jack Donne, and not by D[r] Donne,' Donne tells Carr: 'Reserve it for me, if I live, and if I die, I only forbid it the Presse, and the Fire: publish it not, but yet burn it not.' But there was money in it; and sixteen years after his death, his son gave it to the world.

PAGE 75. A DEFENCE OF WOMEN'S INCONSTANCY. This is the first of the eleven Paradoxes brought together in the volume *Iuvenilia: or certaine Paradoxes, and Problemes, written by I. Donne*, published in 1633. Two others of the Paradoxes concern women; Nos. ii (*That Women ought to paint*), and vi (*That it is possible to find some vertue in some women*). Problem vi raises the question, *Why hath the Common Opinion afforded Women Soules?*—a question with which Donne occupies himself in more than one of his Poems (see, e.g., the poem *To the Countesse of Huntingdon*, 1–4, O.P. p. 177). In l. 20, for *alterable* (1652), 1633 has *intolerable*.

PAGE 78. DONNE'S EARLIEST EXTANT LETTER. The letter belongs pretty certainly to the year 1597, when Donne was employed in the naval expedition which sailed to the Azores under Essex. It was written from Plymouth, where in August the fleet had to shelter from a storm. It has been conjectured that the person to whom the letter is addressed was Donne's friend Christopher Brooke, to whom he sent his poem *The Storme* (O.P. pp. 155–7), and to whom he wrote the lines *To Mr. C. B.* (O.P. p. 184).

l. 11. *ast ego vicissim risero*: the concluding words of Horace, Epode xv. The Burley MS. has *Cicero* for *risero*. See Mrs. Simpson's article in the *Review of English Studies*, April 1944, pp. 224 ff.; the credit of tracing the quotation from Horace belongs to Dr. Paul Maas.

l. 25. *77 Kelleys*: 77 quack alchemists. Edward Kelley, 1555–95, professed to have discovered the Philosopher's Stone; he was imprisoned by the Emperor Rudolf II, and killed while attempting to escape.

PAGE 79. To G. G. See note on *The first Anniversary*, pp. 120–1. G. G. is George Gerard, one of Donne's closest friends, to whom many of his extant letters are addressed. He was a son of Sir William Gerard, of Dooney, Bucks. He became Master of the Charterhouse. In his will, Donne left 'to my kind friend Mr. George Garrard the picture of Mary Magdalene in my chamber'. Among Donne's letters is one to Gerard's sister, Martha (*Letters*, 1651, p. 40).

PAGE 80. To SIR HENRY GOODYERE. This letter is chiefly interesting as showing that, at the end of December 1614, Donne was proposing to print a volume of poems, and to dedicate it to the Lord Chamberlain, Somerset. The book was to be 'a valediction to the world before I take orders'. Within five weeks of writing the letter Donne was, in fact, ordained. If the book was ever printed, the 'few coppies' spoken of must have been very few indeed; no copy has survived, so much as in rumour. Gosse, who is 'convinced that it never existed', supposes that Donne's friends dissuaded him 'from taking the moment of his ordination to publish a collection of his worldly verses which he had never been able to make up his mind as a layman to print'. How 'worldly' the poems were which Donne had in mind to print we have no means of knowing. One poem only does he mention, which he wished to include, the 'Obsequies to the Lord Harington'. This could hardly be styled 'worldly', save as addressed to a person of rank, the Countess of Bedford, and dedicated to the memory of a nobleman, her brother. The book was to contain other pieces addressed to persons of rank. That is all we know of its projected contents. But Gosse speaks as though Donne were publishing *Songs and Sonets*. It seems more likely that what he had in mind was a volume of 'Letters to Severall Personages'. When he speaks of being under 'an unescapable necessity' to print his book (even at his own cost), we may suppose him to mean that he was committed to dedicate something that he had written to Somerset, who was, at the moment, his patron-in-chief.

l. 20. *that good Lady*: the Countess of Bedford.

PAGE 81. 1. *a Rhapsoder*: a stitcher-together; the primitive Greek sense (not, as Gosse takes it, a *ranter*). He is hunting out his poems among the friends to whom he has given copies, in order that he may piece them together in a printed volume. Goodyere seems to have had a good many of them in manuscript, in an 'old book', of which Donne had asked the loan. Goodyere had not sent the book; and it is now, Donne says, too late; for the poems must be printed before he takes orders—it is to be his last lay act. He wishes it to include the *Obsequies* to Harington; because he wants 'something which should bear (the) name' of the Countess of Bedford; the *Obsequies* is not, in fact, a poem addressed to her, but it is *for* her, and is preceded by a prose-letter addressed to her. Donne was careless of his poems, distributing them among his friends, without retaining any copy. We must suppose that, at this date, he had by him none of the seven surviving poems bearing the Countess's name (that none of them had been written seems unlikely). The project of printing is to be kept secret from the Countess; and if Donne cannot use the *Obsequies*, he will be in a difficulty—he cannot write a new poem for his patroness, for in the concluding lines of the *Obsequies* he has vowed a 'sacrifice' to Harington—he has vowed that he will write no more verse:

> Doe not, faire soule, this sacrifice refuse,
> That in my grave I doe interre my Muse,
> Who, by my griefe, great as thy worth, being cast
> Behind hand, yet hath spoke, and spoke her last.

'Behind hand' suggests that the poem was late for its occasion (Harington died on 27 Feb. 1614). Donne had, perhaps, sent it only recently to Goodyere. He wishes to know whether Goodyere has made such use of any part of it that it could not appear in the projected book. He seems to think that Goodyere may have embodied some portion of it in a commemorative collection, or essay, of his own. If he has, even so, Donne thinks, it will not matter; when readers have the whole poem, they will not recognise the excerpt. For his poem, Lady Bedford paid him £30 (*Letters*, 1651, p. 219).

PAGE 81. SERMONS. I. LATE REPENTANCE. Donne was ordained 23 Jan. 1615. He preached his first Sermon, Walton tells us, at Paddington, then a 'village'. This has not survived. His first recorded Sermon, of which an extract is here given, was preached before the Queen at Greenwich, on the third Sunday before Easter (30 April), 1615 (*XXVI Sermons*, pp. 157–8).

PAGE 82. 2. QUEEN ELIZABETH AND KING JAMES. Preached at St. Paul's Cross, 24 March 1617, being the King's Accession-Day (*XXVI Sermons*, pp. 352–3). A letter of John Chamberlain to Sir Dudley Carleton, 29 March 1617, reports 'a Sermon preached before the Archbishop of Canterbury and certain other great Lords at St Paul's Cross, by Dr Donne, who, in the discourse, did Queen Elizabeth *great right*' (*Calendar of State Papers*, James I, 1611–18, p. 454).

PAGE 86. 3. DEATH A RAPTURE AND ECSTASY. Preached to

the Lords, Easter Day (28 March) 1619 (?) (*LXXX Sermons*, pp. 273–4).

PAGE 89. 4. PRAYER. Preached on Candlemas Day (2 Feb.), 1623 (?) (*LXXX Sermons*, pp. 89–90).

PAGE 90. l. 26. some payments you must tender at noon. Hayward's conjecture, 'some of you are too tender' seems unnecessary.

PAGE 93. 5. MERCY AND JUDGMENT. Preached at St. Paul's, on Christmas Day, 1624 (*LXXX Sermons*, pp. 12–13).

PAGE 96. 6. A BETTER RESURRECTION. Preached at St. Paul's, on Easter Day, 25 March 1627 (*LXXX Sermons*, pp. 222–4).

PAGE 100. 7. RELIGIOUS ASSURANCE. Preached at St. Paul's, upon Christmas Day, 1627 (*LXXX Sermons*, pp. 39–40). Coleridge has copied the passage out, beginning from the words 'But as a thoughtfull man . . .', and speaks of it as 'Beautifully imagined and happily applied' (*Literary Remains*, iii, p. 114).

PAGE 101. 8. SIN AND DEATH. Preached before the King at Whitehall, on the first Sunday in Lent (5 March), 1628 (*Fifty Sermons*, pp. 218-19).

PAGE 102. 9. FROM DONNE'S LAST SERMON. For the circumstances, see Walton's *Life*, pp. xxxix–xli. The Sermon was preached before the King at Whitehall, on the first Sunday in Lent (25 Feb.), 1631. On 31 March following, Donne died. The Sermon was printed in 1632, under the title 'Death's Duell'; the title-page states that it was 'called by his Majesties household *The Doctors Owne Funerall Sermon*'.